ESCAPE
101

THE FOUR SECRETS TO TAKING A CAREER BREAK WITHOUT LOSING YOUR MONEY OR YOUR MIND

DAN CLEMENTS & TARA GIGNAC, ND

brainranch
personal & business development publishing

Library and Archives Canada Cataloguing in Publication

Clements, Dan, 1968-
    Escape 101 : the four secrets for taking a career break without losing your money or your mind / Dan Clements & Tara Gignac.

Includes bibliographical references.
Also available in electronic format.
ISBN 978-0-9739782-2-3

    1. Sabbatical leave. 2. Leave of absence. I. Gignac, Tara, 1971-
II. Title. III. Title: Escape one hundred and one.

HD5255.C54 2007   331.25'763   C2007-906179-6

978-0-9739782-2-3 (ISBN 13)

CONTENTS

We must be willing to get rid of the life we've planned, so as to have the life that is waiting for us.

-Joseph Campbell (1904–1987)

Prologue: *Tikal*, Guatemala

THE SPRING OF 1997 found us picking our way through the Guatemalan jungle in near darkness, the forest canopy so dense that the trail was barely visible in the half-light of dawn. As the sky lightened, the screams of howler monkeys began to echo through the vine-hung trees, and we picked up the pace. Our escape—a sabbatical begun the month previous in Mexico—had brought us as far as the ancient Mayan ruins of *Tikal*, and we were determined to reach the top of the much-lauded Temple IV by sunrise.

This wasn't our first extended leave, nor would it be the last. And although this trip would take us to several more Central American countries before we headed home, a chance encounter on this particular day would set us on a path that would wind its way eventually to this book.

We left the main trail and began to work our way uphill, grabbing at roots and vines to keep the pace, pulling ourselves hand over hand up the increasing slope and thickening growth. Just as it seemed we were completely lost, the jungle abruptly ended and we emerged onto the open face of a steep hill.

But it wasn't a hill. The slope we had been climbing was in fact the side of a towering Mayan temple. Its lower portion, the "hill" we had struggled to climb moments before, had been completely reclaimed by jungle and was indistinguishable from the surrounding area. Here, the roots, dirt and undergrowth had been excavated down to stone steps,

ᴇ stood on the ancient temple itself. I paused for a moment to
ᴢ the scene, and then we climbed the remaining distance to the
toₚ, finally pressing our backs against the stone and sidestepping along
a narrow ledge to reach the front of the monolith.

The temple towered over a jungle canopy that stretched, unbroken,
in every direction as far as we could see. As we stood, awed, the sun
rose over thousands of acres of tropical forest. Colorful parrots flew
above the din of the wakening jungle. It was as breathtaking a sight as
I'd seen in all my travels.

As much as that moment has been crystallized in my mind over the
years, it was what happened *next* that would impact the course of our
life together for many years. It would change our family, our work, and
our fortunes. It would start us down a path toward an extraordinary
work-life balance that I am grateful for every single day.

What happened next was simply this: *a family arrived at the top of the
temple.*

It's important to realize that at this time, although we had done
some extensive traveling to various countries, we were relatively young
and unencumbered. Getting away, while challenging, did not involve
mortgages, careers, retirement investments, car payments or businesses.
And it certainly didn't involve children. It involved saving some cash,
quitting (sometimes temporarily, more often permanently) whatever we
were working at and simply *leaving*. Doing that with a family? Well that
was something altogether different.

Wasn't it?

The family that arrived at the top of the temple watched the sunrise
in silence, giving me a chance to observe them. A middle-aged couple
with two pre-teens—young girls, one ten-ish, the other perhaps eight.
Once they'd grown accustomed (as much as was possible) to the
panorama before them, they whispered amongst themselves, shared a
drink of water from their bottle, and turned to greet us.

This family, as it turned out, had been just another typical middle
class family—two kids, two jobs, two cars, one house, one dog, two cats,
living somewhere in suburban America. But that was what they *had*
been. Now, they were something quite different.

The year before, they'd sold everything, pulled the kids out of
school, and were now traveling through Central America, generally
staying a month at a time in a given spot, then moving on. And in their

dramatic break from the "real" world, they felt they truly *had* become something quite different from their demographic equals back home: they had become a happy family.

They were connected. Animated. Curious. Excited. They were all the things I hoped our family would be one day. And even better, they had *escaped*. They'd left it all behind. As far as I could see, they had won the game.

"Was it hard?" I asked the man.

"Leaving?" He smiled and gazed out over the jungle. "Leaving was actually easy. It was *thinking* about leaving that was hard."

We spoke for a while longer, then parted ways to explore the ruins of *Tikal*. And although I never saw them again, I began to see copies of them—cheerful twin-like families that cropped up in our future travels, and resurfaced in memories of trips past. The cyclist couple in New Zealand with their baby in the bike trailer. The young couple camping on the beach in Mexico with their newborn. And it wasn't just families traveling. I saw the same spirit in the people back home who left careers to pursue dreams in business, or to study. To follow their passion, whatever it was.

Everywhere I looked I saw *escapists*. And they all shared two qualities: they were happy, and they were *few*. Though they could be found anywhere, they were an underwhelming minority. They were the cars on the road you never notice until you buy the same model and then see them everywhere.

Years later, as we toured Thailand, Tara pregnant with our daughter, I saw them again, this time appreciating them even more as Tara's belly swelled on the beaches, and our life changed as quickly as the little life that was growing inside her.

But I still wondered. *Why aren't more people doing this?* And I'd think back to the conversation at the top of a Mayan temple years before:

Leaving was actually easy. It was thinking about leaving that was hard.

And so, years later when we took yet another successful sabbatical— this time with jobs, businesses, mortgages and a child—and met still *more* people doing the same thing, a book was born. A book of more than travel advice and tips for saving cash. A book that would make *thinking* about leaving a lot less difficult.

Welcome to *Escape 101*. Your guide to getting away from it all, without giving it all away.

Introduction: Escape is an Inside Job

"What's the world's greatest lie?" the boy asked, completely surprised.

"It's this: that at a certain point in our lives, we lose control of what's happening to us, and our lives become controlled by fate. That's the world's greatest lie."

-Paul Coelho
The Alchemist

ESCAPE ISN'T A NEW idea. From the writings of ancient Greeks, to Thoreau's *Walden*, the idea of pursuing life outside the traditional boundaries has been idealized for centuries. Today, the trend continues still, in modern best-sellers that praise "simple living" or "downsizing".

The tempting premise of getting away from the stress of everyday life hasn't changed much over the years, but one important thing has: it's easier than ever to actually do it.

Or, at least it *should* be easier. Our productivity since World War II has more than doubled. In theory, we should now be able to work half the time, earn the same living our parents did, and spend all that extra time on leisure and other pursuits.

Let's see a show of hands. Who's enjoying their twenty hour work-week? Anyone?

What happened? Instead of exchanging our newfound productivity for time, we've exchanged it for *stuff*.[1] It's as if we've been given a car that's twice as fast, and instead of spending less time driving, we're now choosing a route that's more than twice as long. We're spending just as much time (or more) in the driver's seat, but we're not actually getting anywhere new.

Yet we *want* to get somewhere new.

Almost without exception, everyone I've ever spoken to has expressed an interest in taking extended time off. And they all say the same thing: "I'd love to get away, but I could never do it." The polls support this anecdotal evidence, too. A 2001 survey revealed that more than half the employees of small and midsize companies say they "long" for a sabbatical.[2] People really do want to get away. And not only do they long for it, they even *plan* for it. Statistics from the UK show nearly one in four employees are planning a leave from work in the next 12 months.[3]

The reality though, is that most plans fall short, and we never really do take that dream sabbatical. Why don't we? Why *can't* we? What's stopping us? Hundreds of thousands, perhaps *millions* of people want the experience of a sabbatical, but only a few ever do it. Why?

Why We Don't Take The Time We Need

A recent study claimed that over half of Americans fail to use all their vacation time.[4] And that's just one study—statistics consistently show that North Americans are taking fewer and fewer vacations, and working longer hours. So not only are we not taking extended time away from work, but many of us aren't taking *any* time away. And if we do, it's not real vacation. We check email, carry cell phones, and take conference calls. We fret and worry. We try to jam so much into our short vacation that we end up coming home more stressed out than we were before we left.

But we need the time. We want the time. Studies suggest we would trade *money* for the time. Economics says it should be easy to escape, and there's no shortage of people who want to, so why isn't it happening? Are we truly trapped by the choices we've made? By our career progress, our mortgages, our retirement savings, our businesses and family obligations?

The answer is no. The reality is not that people *don't get away* (although they don't). The truth is that people *won't get away*. They won't take the simple steps necessary to make it happen—to recover their health, their families, and themselves. We'll get into the reasons why in more detail, but for now understand this: *Although it's not easy to leave your life, it's by no means impossible*. In fact, as you'll discover in this book, it's really not that hard at all.

Leaving the rat race is not as daunting as it may seem. You'll look back in later years and marvel at how easy it was and how much you gained for so little cost. It is however, fraught with potential pitfalls. Fortunately most, if not all, are avoidable with a little planning.

Ironically, however, the first pitfall is planning itself. It's easy to pull out the calculator from under your stack of monthly bills and start to calculate the cost of taking a year off—the cost of leaving and traveling, the opportunity cost of a year without working, the loss of forward momentum in your business or career, to name a few. The trap that awaits you here, though, is that you'll likely scare yourself into quiet, hiatus-free submission for the rest of your life. Or what ultravagabond Tim Ferriss, author of *The 4-Hour Workweek*, calls dying a "slow spiritual death over 30-40 years of tolerating the mediocre."[5] Ouch.

Do you need a plan? Sure. Do you need to make the plan *first*? No. *Extended time off is a mental game*. It's a challenge of mind and heart, not of storage lockers and checkbooks. Before you can dive into the details of your sabbatical, you need to become master of your own thoughts and emotions.

As a species we've gone to the moon, eradicated diseases, and designed incredible technologies and feats of architecture, all of which started as *thoughts*. The four secrets that follow are about shaping your mind, your beliefs, and your attitudes. They're about shaping your thinking, so that you can shape your world.

You're about to discover the four simple secrets that change *won't* into *will*.

What This Book Will Do For You

There are other sabbatical books out there. I think they're all excellent, and I've included a recommended reading list at the end. I can, however, tell you that this one is a bit different.

There are as many different ways to enjoy a sabbatical as there are excuses to not take one. While every sabbatical is unique in its own way, the excuses all share one thing: *they're all in your head.* Time away, living your life the way you've dreamed of, is real. The reasons you may be afraid to do it aren't.

The challenge, though, is that the mental roadblocks to getting away *seem* real. Incredibly real. More real than actually getting away. This book is about dealing with those demons first. About playing the *inner game* of sabbatical planning first, to borrow a phrase from W. Timothy Gallwey.[6]

This book represents your first step towards choosing your life the way you want it.

Taking time off from your life doesn't require as much money as you think, nor is it really that hard. It takes some guts, though, and a small dose of wisdom. This book will help with both.

Beyond marking the starting point in what I hope will be an incredible journey for you, here's what this book can help you do:

- Find the motivation to follow your dream of taking time off
- Commit to your sabbatical in small, easy steps that will ensure you really do get away
- Take action on the critical elements of your "escape plan"
- Manage money so that you have plenty when you go
- Leave without going broke
- Leave your job without losing career progress
- Take a year off without sacrificing your savings or investments
- Successfully pitch your sabbatical to your boss
- Be away from your business for extended periods of time, and still remain profitable
- Take a year off on a shoestring budget
- Make money or even get paid while you're gone
- Be financially independent for a year or more
- Plan all of your sabbatical finances in just 30 minutes

Is this book just for travelers? No. If you want to take time away from the pressures of career or business for any reason, this book's for you. It is, however, written from the perspective of getting *away*. Travel—or at least "changing locations"—for the duration of your sabbatical has some additional benefits that we'll discuss, but if your plan is to write a book, go back to school, or any number of other things that don't involve leaving your home, rest assured you've still come to the right place.

It's Not About the Money

For most people, the idea of leaving work or business for more than two weeks goes beyond excuses; it seems *impossible*. They don't *believe* they can do it. They think sabbaticals are for other people. People with unusual combinations of talent, guts, money, time, and jobs.

And more often than not, they think they're for the wealthy.

It's not true. Backpacking college grads would seem to outnumber 'grownups' on the long-term leave trail by a factor of 50:1, and they're notoriously broke. Not only is being wealthy not a requirement, but in many ways it becomes *harder* to take time off as your level of wealth increases. The wealthier you are, the more you have to lose. As your net worth climbs, your life is supported by an increasing infrastructure—things like cars, cottages, homes and boats that become anchors to the status quo. The higher you climb, the further you can fall, if you believe the old adage.

If you're wealthy, don't let this stop you. This book's going to help you just as much. But more importantly, know this: if you're *not* independently wealthy—if you've got a job, a career, a business or if you're unemployed and broke—*you can take a sabbatical.* You might not think so right now, but that's okay. My job is to convince you, and give you the simple tools required to get away, wealthy or not.

Taking a sabbatical is also more than getting away from the pressures of life or seeing the world. It's more than doing some good somewhere, or learning a skill you've always longed to master. And yes, it's much more than leaving a job you can't stand (although that's a heck of a compelling motive).

Your sabbatical is about doing what *you* want. It's about living your life in alignment with your heart. It's about dancing to the music that makes your heart sing.

Your sabbatical is about *living deliberately.*

When you start to live your life on purpose, you discover that there's a whole other side of you that's been locked away for years. Your sabbatical is about releasing that side. It's about unlocking the part of you that you know is still there, but may have been afraid to acknowledge.

The first step to unlocking that hidden side is to recognize one thing: everything you need to exit the rat race and take extended time off from your life is *inside you.* Like most things of true value, the sabbatical game is played mainly in the mind. Like the perfect heist, escaping your "normal" life is an inside job.

Before We Begin

This book is about the hard part of leaving your life (that *thinking* part). Its argument goes roughly like this:

1. Most people want to take a sabbatical or career break, but don't.
2. The reasons people don't are really mental/emotional, not practical or logistical. They're abstract things like fear and uncertainty, not cash flow or seniority.
3. There is a solution to this.

This isn't a backpacking guide for gap-year college students. With youth comes a natural ability to see past obstacles, and for most of the mortgage- and kid-free crowd, escape isn't a hopeful luxury. It's an inborn *talent.*

Unlike most other talents, however, that natural hedonism fades over time, and talent is slowly replaced by *tolerance.* We accept that our role is to aim for some distant, speculative finish line when we'll have the resources to escape, and we put our heads down and toe the line.

This book is about changing that route to the finish line—at least for a few months—without changing the actual finish line itself. It's about taking the break you need, without losing ground. More precisely, it's about taking three months to a year off, without burning your career, business, relationships and savings to the ground.

Before we get started, I'm going to ask you to make two important commitments: They're neither difficult nor time-consuming, but they do require a certain attitude shift.

Here's the first: *suspend your disbelief.*

When you watch a great film, you do this almost subconsciously. You "forget" that the people are actors, that the setting is a set. In fact, just out of your view (the camera's view, actually) an entire infrastructure of equipment and personnel is engaged solely in ensuring that you immerse yourself in a brand new world so completely that it becomes real.

So for now, do the same as you would during a night at the movies and suspend your disbelief. Choose to be open to the *possibility* of a hiatus from your normal life. Remove "can't" and "impossible" from your vocabulary long enough to give the idea a chance. Allow yourself to exit the rat race mentally for now, safe in the knowledge that dreaming is cost-free, and you can turn back at any time.

The second commitment is easier, since it requires you to *not* do something. It's this: *stop planning.*

Before you assume this is dead easy, however, take note. Just below the surface of your consciousness, your remarkable brain is operating an auto-planning, predicting mechanism that constantly calculates next steps, likelihood of success, and more importantly, whether we should even *bother* with something.

This system is running all the time, even in your sleep, and it's this mechanism that tends to throw ideas out the window before we get a chance to really consider them, often in conversations that look something like this:

You: *I'd love to take a sabbatical. Okay. First I'll need to talk to management, and get some money together, then -*

Your brain (interrupting): *You can't afford it, and your boss will never let you.*

You: *Yeah. Even if the boss would let me, I could never afford it.*

What's really happening here? Your brain immediately starts predicting and planning. In an instant, two big roadblocks—jobs and finances—appear on the radar, and the idea is shut down without further consideration. It's all over in a few synaptic blinks.

While it's difficult to turn off your brain, you can start by refusing to actively plan—at least until you get to the planning part of the book. Forget about trying to imagine where the money will come from, and how you can break the news to your boss, employees, colleagues or friends. Stop planning. Stop wondering *how*, and open your mind to enjoying *what* your time away could be, and *why* it's important.

Trust in this: there is a *how*, and it's in this book, but we're not going there first. We'll get to how eventually, but as the man says, we've got bigger fish to fry.

It's time to *escape*.

PART 1: The 4 Secrets for Getting Away From It All

"I can't believe impossible things." said Alice.
"I daresay you haven't had much practice," said the Queen. "When I was your age, I always did it for half-an-hour a day. Why, sometimes I've be-lieved as many as six impossible things before breakfast."

-Lewis Carroll
Alice's Adventures in Wonderland

THE FIRST SECRET: DESIRE

Finding a powerful "why".

Dwell not upon thy weariness, thy strength shall be according to the measure of thy desire.

- Arab Proverb

YOU'RE READING A BOOK about how to dramatically change your life. Just the simple action of buying this book and sitting down to read it puts you ahead of 99% of the millions and millions of people who would like to take extended time off from their lives, but aren't doing anything about it. That one simple step has revealed something important: *there's a desire in you to change the way things are.*

In fact, fanning that desire is the first step in making your sabbatical dream a reality. Welcome to the first secret of getting away: the secret of *Desire.*

How Desire Works

Desire is different from *want*. Desire is want on steroids. Desire is a want that has become so compelling, that it becomes a *need*. Desire is a passion so strong that it overcomes any obstacle life might throw in the way. Lots of people *want* to escape. The ones who *must* are the ones who will.

Think about your sabbatical dreams. What's stopping you from leaving tomorrow, or next week? Is it lack of money? Fear of leaving your job? Those are all valid concerns, but what would happen if someone put a gun to your head? Would you suddenly find the drive to make it happen? My guess is that the answer is yes. Your *want* would have suddenly become a *need*. You'd hop on a plane faster than you could say "take this job and shove it". Having a gun to your head would have very suddenly and radically shifted your priorities.

The challenge (thankfully) in daily life is that there is no one with a gun to your head. While this has its benefits, it also leaves you in the position of having to find other ways to move from *want* to *need*. Fortunately, the strategies for building desire do exist, and they're a lot more positive.

Much has been made of goal-setting in self-development literature. Workshops, books, audiobooks and even software programs have been developed to help people identify goals and take steps to achieve them. If one constant has emerged from decades of research and writing on the topic, though, it's that achieving any goal that you're not emotionally attached to is very difficult. And not much fun either.

Very few people will achieve goals simply because they set them. If you don't have a *desire* for the goal you've set, the odds of achieving it are greatly reduced.

To make your sabbatical dreams a reality, you'll need to become emotionally attached to it. You'll need to make your *wants* into *needs*. Your *shoulds* into *musts*. Your *mights* into *wills*.

Finding Desire Part 1: Your Sabbatical Type

Although you might find this book in the how-to section, the *why*-to part of escaping the rat race is just as critical, if not more so, than the how.

With a strong enough why—a compelling reason to leave—you'll almost always find a how. If you're motivated (if your *desire* is strong) your brain will find a way to reach your goal.

The first step in building your desire—in making your goal as compelling and emotionally charged as possible—is to discover your *why*. What is it about time away that's so compelling for you? What's your personal reason for wanting to take a sabbatical? Why do you want to go?

In reality, there are as many unique reasons to go as there are people who want to. With so many possible reasons why, how do you find yours? To shed some light on the seeds of desire, let's take a look at four personality types of people who want to pack up and get away from it all.

Escape Artists

Escape Artists are perhaps the most common type of sabbatical-seeker. The idea of getting away from a job, a relationship, or a certain environment is a compelling one, and a sabbatical provides a great excuse. It's easy to say, "I'm leaving my job because I'm doing volunteer work in Africa." It's a lot harder to say, "I'm leaving my job because I don't like it, I'm not fulfilled, and I don't know what I'm going to do with myself."

Escape Artists tend to be moving away from something, as opposed to going toward something. They truly want to "get away". If you dream of quitting your job and not having to deal with your nemesis in the next cubicle, or the overbearing boss, then you're an escape artist. Your job here is to master the art of doing it.

Explorers

Finding something new. Exploring the unexplored. To bravely go where no man...well, you get the picture. Discovery is a powerful motivator for some. While many people thrive on security, Explorers want to find what's new, what they've never tried, and what's never been seen.

If you're an Explorer, you like the idea of trying new foods, seeing new places—even if the new place is only in the next town over. You're not put off by the thought of travel. All the sitting, waiting, sweating of travel? It's all just part of the buzz of trying something new. Unlike

Escape Artists, you're motivated more by the great pyramids than by the great escape. It's where you're headed, not where you've been.

You're also not afraid of change, although for the Explorers who haven't traveled beyond the Discovery channel for a few years, it may take you some time to get back in gear. Don't worry—we're in baby step mode. It's just like riding a bike, only you don't even have to know how in the first place. It'll come naturally to you.

Growers

While Explorers want to learn more about the world, Growers want to learn more about themselves. If you're a Grower, your sabbatical might be about things like learning a new skill, finding your place in the world, learning a language, or "finding yourself". Growers are into personal development. They want to take time off to find or improve themselves. If you're a Grower, your time away is often about *you*.

But Growers aren't just selfish and self-absorbed. Many Growers are taking time away to build a stronger relationship with those closest to them—new babies, spouses, family and intimate friends. For Growers, the point of getting away is to *improve* something.

Recoverers

While Escape Artists tend to have a personality that makes them want to get away from things, Recoverers need to get away for very concrete, external reasons—something in their life is driving them away. A failed relationship, a serious illness, job burnout, or loss of a loved one will send some people into recovery mode. If you're a Recoverer, you need some space and time to put the pieces back together.

Which One are You?

Don't feel you fit any of these categories? You may fit more than one, or even all of them. The point is that knowing your sabbatical "type" may help you decide more precisely *why* you want to take time away.

Start by choosing the type that describes your motivation for wanting to escape. Even if you feel that *all* of the types apply, start by choosing the one that fits you *best*.

What is it about this type that strikes a chord with you?

Finding Desire Part 2: Your Powerful *Why*

Strong reasons make strong actions.

-William Shakespeare

If you've got an idea of what your sabbatical type is, then let's dig in a bit more to your specific motivation for wanting to take an extended leave. Like your sabbatical type, you may find that more than one of the following appeals to you. In fact, once you get the sabbatical "bug" they *all* seem pretty appealing. Don't let that worry you, though—more desire is better than less!

Work Related

Perhaps the most common reason people give for wanting to take a sabbatical is work-related. They simply want to leave their jobs.

Job burnout has become a common phenomenon. Phrases like 'stress leave' that barely existed a few decades ago, now seem to be common parlance. The rat race. The treadmill. The daily grind. They're all terms to describe stress-filled work lives that seem to be, for many, devoid of purpose.

Getting away from it all is linked to escaping from work for good reason. Most people simply will not give themselves permission to stop working. They either won't allow it, or are too scared to believe they can do it. Planning a *sabbatical*, however, gives them a reason to leave work—a guilt-free excuse, you might say.

There's nothing wrong with that. Remember—we're looking for your *trigger*. What is the one reason that will ignite your passion to get outta here? If escaping from work is your trigger, then so be it.

If you're in the position of disliking, or being overwhelmed by your job, just imagine if you *didn't* have to get up for work tomorrow. Imagine if the deadlines, pressures and conflicts of everyday work simply...vanished. What if you could get up tomorrow morning, and do *whatever you wanted?*

The truth is you can. And whether you love or hate your work, taking a sabbatical can have a profound impact on your professional life. You can recover from job burnout, or advance your knowledge in your area of expertise by going back to school. You can rediscover what you once loved about your job, or discover a brand new type of work that's more rewarding. You can recharge, rebalance and then return to the same thing, or move on to something entirely different. The choice is yours.

Health

As a species, we've been moving to new places to improve our health for as long as we've had health to worry about. Our earliest ancestors were hunters and gatherers and nomads. Seasonal, or even constant relocation, was a simple fact of life: you move somewhere new, or you die.

While we no longer need to pack up our homes in order to find food, relocation can have profound effect on physical and mental health. For centuries, doctors have prescribed relocation as a panacea for everything from Tuberculosis to Touret's Syndrome. And while it's no miracle cure for everyone, people return from sabbaticals dramatically, physically changed. Free of the rigors of daily life, able to pursue their dreams, escapists lose weight, escape depression, and develop that energetic "glow" that's unique to the pregnant and truly happy.

Spending time doing what you truly love is a remarkable experience, one that's reflected in your health and well-being.

Volunteer/Contribute

Volunteering could well be the quintessential sabbatical experience. It's almost a stereotype: khaki-clad workers laboring in the hot sun to provide medical care, drill wells, teach, or build churches.

There's a good reason for this image, though: it's common, and it's rewarding. There's something incredibly refreshing to do work for something more than money. Even if it's only a short part of your sabbatical, a volunteer experience can change your life.

Bear in mind that volunteering doesn't have to happen in a third-world country. There are opportunities all over the world, from the wealthiest to the poorest nations, to give something of yourself.

Travel/Adventure

Some of us just have the travel bug. For the cubicle dreamers, "exotic" can mean just about anywhere, as long as it's not here.

Travel offers boundless opportunities for fresh perspective on your "regular" life. New cultures, languages, peoples and locales are an eye-opening benchmark against which to compare everything that you consider normal.

Most people have a dream destination. France. Italy. Fiji. Cleveland. What's yours? What destination makes you sit up straighter in your chair when you think of it? What one postcard would you hang on your cubicle wall?

How about exotic activities? Mountain climbing? Bunjee jumping? If you could snap your fingers and transport yourself to anywhere in the world, where would it be? The great pyramids? Antarctica? The South Pacific?

For many of us, the seeds of our dream destination were planted as children in the books we read, the movies we watched and the games we played. Think back to that time. What did you dream of as a child? Where did you want to go? What did you want to do?

What's your dream destination?

Family/Relationships

For many, today's relative affluence has come at a cost far beyond the sticker price of the new car in our driveway. Long working hours, and two-income families have changed, often for the worst, the fabric of how we interact with children, spouses, extended family, and friends.

Time away from the pressures of everyday life allow us to reconnect with loved ones in ways we may have forgotten, or never experienced at all.

Self-Awareness

'Finding yourself' has been a common phrase for several decades. It's tossed around pretty freely to describe the aimless wanderings of post-college backpackers, but it's a valid purpose for taking time away.

How much time have you set aside in the past year just for *you*? Time where you had no obligations or interruptions? And even if you have set aside such time, were you able to fully enjoy it, without the feeling that you should be doing something else?

And finally, even if you *have* carved out a chunk of sacred time, how much of that time was spent considering...you? Looking at what makes you truly happy? Thinking about your future? Contemplating your life and your contributions? If you're like most people, chances are that you haven't spent much time at all doing those things. One of the magical experiences of a hiatus is the ability to free your mind of clutter and consider your life outside of the context of your regular routine.

Just imagine the pure, guilt-free joy of time for *you*. Time to grow, rediscover, or reinvent yourself. When was the last time you had *that* in abundance?

Perspective

I've always considered this the greatest gift of taking extended time off. Removed from the pace and obligations of everyday life, you're able to see things in an entirely different way than you normally would. It can lead to some poignant and even shocking insights about the life you lead.

It's difficult to describe the sensation of looking at your life as if it's not yours. In the same way that it can seem so easy to help someone *else* solve a problem or choose a course of action, a long absence from your "normal" life provides almost the same ability. You'll find a new clarity in how you see your life that you might never have found without leaving it.

Wealth

It wasn't that long ago that young people set off into the world to "find their fortune". Somewhere between then and now, though, we gave up the idea of leaving home in search of wealth and fame, and began embarking on stable careers with secure paychecks. Somehow, we became convinced that the pot of gold was at the top of the corporate ladder, not at the end of the rainbow.

At first glance, wealth may seem like the last thing that would appear on a list of reasons for taking a sabbatical. After all, doesn't a sabbatical *decrease* your wealth? Decreased income, added travel expenses, lost earning time—how can taking time off increase your wealth?

We'll get into this in more detail in a later section, but for now, suffice it to say that taking a sabbatical is *not* a one-way route to poverty. Not only does it not have to decrease your wealth, but it could make you financially better off than you are now. No kidding. For the moment, just open your mind to the idea that extended time off and wealth are not incompatible ideas. And this holds true whether you own a business, have a career, or are unemployed.

Exiting the rat race has yet another unexpected bonus: it can greatly enhance your financial IQ. As you'll discover in the chapter on money, the acts of saving, prioritizing, focusing, investing, managing real estate, and assessing risk are all part of a good sabbatical plan. What's interesting is that it just so happens that they're all an essential part of financial health for the rest of your life, too.

Change

There's much truth in the saying, "a change is as good as a rest". Strangely, though, we spend much of our lives doing everything we can to avoid change. We cling to the lifeline of routine as tightly as possible, but still find ourselves unrested and unfulfilled.

Change for the sake of change is a fine reason to plan a hiatus. If your only reason for taking a sabbatical is the nagging voice that tells you "I need a change", you could do worse. Change for the sake of change is fine change indeed.

Growth/Learning

Sabbaticals bring change in abundance, and with change comes growth. Whether you want to learn a new language, study physics or learn to meditate, extended time away provides ample opportunity to learn. Not only will you find it easier to create the time to learn, you'll find you can do it more quickly and easily.

And whether you consciously desire it or not, personal growth is a natural result of sabbaticals. Even if it's not your goal, you'll find it inevitable.

Recovery

Life happens despite our best intentions. Sometimes, unfortunate circumstances even happen *because* of them. Whatever the reason, crippling emotional events are a part of life, and although "normal" life routines can be helpful in getting through times of distress, they can also stand in the way of long-term healing—physical and emotional.

A significant change of life can bring with it remarkable healing. Loss of a loved one, divorce and other emotional traumas can be more easily resolved through the distance of time away from the circumstances in which they occurred. Those who've followed their passion often move past emotional and physical problems without realizing it—

it's only when reminded by someone else that they recall their previous discomfort.

A hiatus can be a panacea unlike anything you might have experienced. Don't shrug off the idea simply because of your present circumstances.

Love

Looking for love in all the wrong places? For most people in search of that special someone, the real problem is looking for love in hardly *any* places. The average person today needs to find romance within a few departments of his cubicle, or he isn't going to find it at all. That can make for limited choice.

One of the great joys of extended time away from normal life is the number and diversity of people that you'll encounter along the way. Add to that the joyful, stress-reduced environment of a sabbatical, and you've got the perfect breeding ground for relationships. And while most of us don't readily admit we're looking for love, subconsciously we all crave it and the more people we meet under joyful circumstances, the more likely we are to find it.

Meaning

There's a Bizarro comic that always struck me as poignant. An old man lays on his death bed. Surrounded by friends and family, he's reflecting on his life accomplishments. He says, "I watched a lot of TV, ate a lot of fast food, and sold more laminated countertops in June of 1973 than anyone else in the Southeast region. My work here is done."

An exaggeration? Perhaps. Thought provoking? Most certainly. It's a spin on the lack of substance in our lives, and it hits close to home because deep inside, most of us worry that we're going to end up with a life story just like his.

We all long to be part of something bigger. From the first sparks of intelligence in early man, we've struggled to make sense of the world around us—to explain the unexplainable. To find our role in the 'big scheme of things'. If something tugs at your insides - if a small voice inside you says, "there's more than just this" - then you may very well be searching for meaning.

It can be a challenge to find meaning in daily life. The current pace of things makes it difficult to get your kids to school, never mind reflect on the grand machinery of the universe. The search for meaning, like all good searches, requires some time and dedication. That's hard to come by these days, but it's available by the bucketful when you take a sabbatical.

If meaning is your only motivation for making this change in your life, you could do far worse. You're in the company of kings and philosophers, poets and scientists, the best of which searched for - and sometimes found - meaning. Yes, you could definitely do worse.

ॐ

At the root of so many of these reasons for wanting to take time away is time, or lack of it. Imagine for a moment that your lifespan is 1000 years, instead of 60-100. How would that affect your approach to work? To relationships? To goals and wants?

The perceived shortage of time in our lives manifests itself in many different ways. It's the alarm clock that wakes us with less sleep than we should have. It's the vacation cut short or cancelled. It's a bizarre series of chronic health problems. Time shortage, paradoxically, even causes us to waste *more* time on activities that don't add much value to our lives—watching excessive TV, for example. In an effort to escape from our perceived lack of time, we waste more time. It's no wonder we feel like rats on a treadmill.

But we're not dumb. We want our time back. According to a 2007 survey, a *quarter* of employees would take a cut in pay of more than 15 percent to gain an extra hour a day with family and loved ones.[7] So, in yet another paradox, we're willing to pay to get the time back that we traded for money in the first place!

Tim Kasser, a psychology professor at Knox College in Illinois is the author of *The High Price of Materialism*. He's done considerable research into consumer culture and its impact on our lives, and found people who are "time affluent" are happier than those who are materially affluent. To put it more simply: those with time, are happier than those with money.

But don't we all have the same amount of time?

I use the phrase *perceived shortage of time* for good reason. Every single one of us has 24 hours in a day. It's the one constant we all share.

We may come from different socio-economic backgrounds, and have different skills, abilities and opportunities, but without exception, every single one of us has a 365-day year at our disposal. Despite how it may seem to a single mother working in corporate law, she has precisely the same number of hours in a day as the retired dot-com millionaire.

So how does taking time away give us our time back?

Most obviously, we're carving it out for ourselves—creating large blocks of that ethereal stuff we call "time" to be used for our own delicious, selfish, pleasurable purposes. When you take a sabbatical, you manage time in large amounts, instead of it managing you. That's something that just doesn't happen enough.

Less obvious, but more important, are the secondary effects of carving out this extra time. Time away grants you the perspective of being on the other side of the fence. After all, you can't know sad without happy, and the same applies to *busy*. Sabbaticals grant you a new set of eyes with which to view your current life. Better yet, you get to keep your old eyes so you can compare experiences when you return.

And what's more, you may find yourself more empowered to take control of your time more often. If you've done it once, you can do it again. And again. Your time truly becomes *yours* to use.

Escape artists often find a whole range of unexpected benefits that propagate from taking control of their time. New careers. Increased wealth and health. Intangibles like courage, joy, and fulfillment that are inexplicably linked to the simple decision to create six months of time that is yours and yours alone.

☙

Earlier I discussed how straightforward it would be to change your life if someone put a gun to your head. Not a pretty picture, but an effective one nonetheless. The reality, however, is that there *isn't* a gun to your head. You can always put off your sabbatical for another day.

In the world of "sabbaticalists", this is a dangerous prospect.

There's a fable about frogs and hot water that goes like this: drop a frog in a pot of boiling water and it will immediately hop right back out. Put the frog in a pot of cool water, and he'll sit there contentedly.

Put that pot on the stove and *slowly* turn up the heat, and legend has it that the frog will stay in the pot and slowly cook to death.

What kills the frog? Why doesn't he just hop out?

What gets the frog in the end is the *rate* of change. The frog continues to adjust to the increasing temperature. Sure it's hot, but he gets used to it. It gets hotter still, but he gets used to that, too. Then, in one instant, it's *too* hot, and the frog dies.

Let's be clear: I'm not calling you a frog. I'm sure you're quite attractive. What I am saying is that life can be a slow pressure cooker. You get a job, and it's hard at first, but you get used to it. You get a mortgage and kids. Life gets busy, but it happens slowly, and you adapt. You get a promotion, and with it comes more work, but you adapt. You need a little more money all the time to pay for your growing life, so you work a little harder, but it's okay because you adapt, and hey, life is pretty good, no?

At the same time, though, the slow creep is happening in other ways. Maybe you've gained an extra four or five pounds a year for the last decade, and suddenly you're 50 pounds overweight. Your arteries aren't quite the shiny new pipes they used to be. Worse still, you haven't had a good, honest laugh with your spouse in years. And you haven't had sex in months. And it gets worse. When was the last time you felt filled with possibility? With joy?

It's that aforementioned incredible ability to *tolerate* that's letting things sneak up on you. The pot's heating up. And the tragedy is that one minute you're busy enjoying the water, and the next minute you're dead. Like the frog, it's easy to miss the signals that the path you're on could have an abrupt end.

What's changed in your life over the years? How have *you* changed? Has it been too subtle to notice?

So yes, there is no gun to your head. But for many of us, the heat that's building up in our lives is a slow gun swinging in our direction. It takes years for the barrel to make its way around, but only an instant to pull the trigger. It takes ages for the pot to heat up, but once it reaches critical temperature, it's all over in an instant.

Desire is your starting point for becoming aware that the water in the pot is heating up, and that maybe, just maybe, there could be something better out there. Desire is your first step to climbing out of the pot.

And please, make sure you bring the frog with you when you go. It's hot in there, man.

Cଓ

Desire is the engine that will power your drive to get away from it all. Desire is your strong *why*, and if it's strong enough, it will help you find all the *how* you need.

Most people begin their sabbatical journey with a motivating reason—like wanting to escape their work, or visit another country. Along the way, however, many realize that the *reason* they wanted to get away from it all is not the entire picture. The benefits of leaving your job to travel are not limited to sleeping in, or not having to deal with Stanley in the next cubicle. They're limitless. You could experience any or even all of the benefits mentioned here, or countless others not discussed.

Just remember that your Desire—the drive that starts your sabbatical quest—is only the tip of the iceberg. Like most people, your sabbatical is likely to take you to insights and rewards beyond what you imagine right now. For the moment, though, fuel up your passion and let the rest fall into place.

To help build that desire, go back over the list of reasons for taking a sabbatical. Which one appeals most to you? Is it the delicious pleasure of waking up in a hammock under a coconut tree, and realizing you don't have to go to work for a whole *year*? The inspiration of finally getting to write that book you always dreamed of? Sipping wine with your spouse in some of the finest vineyards in the world?

One (or more) of these—or one that's not even on the list—will appeal to you more than the others. It's probably one that you knew before you even opened this book. Latch onto it. Imagine the feeling of being right there. Smell the air. Taste the food.

Now hold that thought. It's time for the next step.

THE SECOND SECRET: BELIEF

Actually, you can.

Belief creates the actual fact....the greatest revolution of my generation is the discovery that individuals, by changing their inner attitudes of mind, can change the outer aspects of their lives.

-Dr. William James, Harvard Psychologist

O N MAY 6TH, 1954, a young medical student named Roger Bannister completed his patient rounds before heading to the rough athletic track at Oxford University for an event that would make history. At stake was a world record for running a single mile set by Gunder Haegg, a Swede who'd held the coveted position for over nine years with a time of 4 minutes, 1.4 seconds.

The day was rainy and windy—conditions that could cost a runner several seconds of precious time—but his coach encouraged him nonetheless. He knew Bannister wasn't just out to break the world record. He was setting out to break the "four-minute barrier". Running a mile in under four minutes was a feat considered impossible by many, and for some, marked an actual physical limit for the human body. For the athletes themselves, even if they felt their physical body capable of such a feat, the four-minute mile presented an insurmountable mental barrier. The best in the world could get close—repeatedly—but never quite *past*.

Bannister, however, just couldn't seem to see the psychological side of the challenge. It made no sense to him that you could get that close to a four-minute mile, but not get past it.[8]

The gun sounded. A few very short minutes later, Bannister was swarmed by over a thousand spectators after doing just what he had set out to do: break the four-minute mile, with a time of 3 minutes, 59.4 seconds.

By all accounts, Bannister's feat was a wonder. His training was far less intense than that of today's milers. The track was made of cinder, the shoes and clothing "old-fashioned" and decidedly low-tech by today's standards. What makes the story truly remarkable, however, is not Bannister's performance under these conditions. What makes it remarkable is that his performance was bested by nearly 2 seconds just 56 days later by another runner! And in the next three years, *fifteen more* runners would go on to break the unbreakable four-minute barrier.

Bannister's feat did one simple thing: he proved it was *possible*. And once he proved it, others thought so, too. Based on Bannister's proof, they began to *believe*.

Today, the four-minute mile still represents a standard for all top runners, but no one doubts its achievability. It's now simply a benchmark.

CƷ

Whether you believe you can or you can't, you're right.

-Henry Ford

Henry Ford's statement is referenced so frequently it's almost a cliché. As with many clichés, though, there's good reason for its overuse: it's *true*.

There are many people who have the first secret nailed: they really do have the *desire* to get away. They really want to go on sabbatical. They want it so badly they can taste it. So what's holding them back?

The truth is that they simply don't believe they can. In most people's minds, sabbaticals are the purview of the rich, the crazy, or the brave. After all, you'd have to be at least one of those three to give up a perfectly good job and move to France to learn to cook, wouldn't you? *Wouldn't you?*

No. Sorry to disappoint you, but taking a year off is more than possible for anyone. As a matter of fact, if you can afford to buy this book, you can take a year off.

This one's worth repeating: *if you can afford to buy this book, you can take a year off.*

We'll get into money later—for now, let's just play hardball and say that it's not a valid excuse. Right now, accept that in order to pull this off you'll need to *believe* you can.

The truth of this statement comes from the thousands of people who've taken time off from their lives, and lived and prospered to tell the tale. They are people just like you. As a matter of fact, right this minute, someone with less money than you is taking six months to tour Europe. What's the difference between them and you? It's not socio-economic status. It's not brains. It's not bravery. The difference between them and you is that they wanted to, they believed they could, and so they did. Simple as that.

As Timothy Ferriss says in *The 4-Hour Workweek:* "I've since met paraplegics and the deaf, senior citizens and single mothers, home owners and the poor, all of whom have sought and found excellent life-changing reasons for extended travel instead of dwelling on the million small reasons *against* it."

So how do you start to believe *you* can do the same thing? Let's start by looking at why you *don't* believe you can do it. Lack of belief has three distinct sources:

1. Lack of Experience

If you've never taken extended time off, and you've never had someone tell you how to do it, then simple lack of experience could be holding you back.

Many things were unattainable until someone else did them. Landing on the moon, breaking the four-minute mile—they were all thought to be *impossible* until someone did it. And once someone did it, the feat was promptly repeated many times over.

Understand that many, many thousands of people have done this. They've blazed an easy-to-follow trail. And luckily, some of them have documented it—one of the best reasons for reading some of the books in the reading section at the end of *Escape 101* is to discover even more stories from successful escapists. The more you read, the more you realize that while you are special—uniquely so—your circumstances are not. Many people with very similar lives have taken time off to follow their dreams. If they can do it, so can you. All you need is this book and a little homework.

2. It's against the status quo

Let's face it: life, as far as most people are concerned, is very prescriptive. You get a job, hang onto it as best you can, and try to retire someday. Now, there's nothing wrong with that, it's just that it's what *everyone* does. Your decision to leave work is not *normal* in the eyes of the majority. People may think you're weird. Or crazy. Or both.

If this bothers you, take solace in this fact: the people doing the "normal" stuff are often just jealous. As mentioned earlier, most working stiffs have a secret desire to get away from it all. *They just don't know how.* Now that you're learning how, don't be surprised to find yourself slowly detaching from the status quo. As we'll see, that may provoke some unusual responses. Don't worry, that's *normal.* For them.

Normal is really another way of saying *average.* It's amazing how many people want to be normal, but nobody ever seems to want to be average. A sabbatical is a way to become a leader in your own life instead of hanging with the pack. It's a way to follow your own dreams instead of someone else's.

Taking time off is a way for you to become *extraordinary.*

3. It provides an excuse

While lack of belief, or "can't" is a common reason for not getting away, there's more to "can't" than meets the eye. For many people, the various barriers to sabbaticals—money, jobs, kids, etc.—are actually convenient excuses. They provide an easy way out of dealing with something even scarier: the truth.

For every dream of getting away, there's a corresponding thought that goes something like this: *what if I love it, and realize that this other life I'm living is a sham?* Planning a sabbatical plants the seeds of doubt. What if we really don't like our jobs? Or our lives? Our homes? Our *friends?*

This is normal, too. And while a sabbatical may hold up a mirror to your life that shows things to be not as you thought they were, that same mirror puts an even brighter shine on the things in your life that truly are important, and that you really do value. My guess is you'll come back from your sabbatical with your head screwed on exactly right—loving what you really love, and disinterested in what you don't.

All these reasons for not believing you can take a sabbatical are really fear-based. What will people think? What if I don't have enough money? What if something bad happens? What if I can't find a job when I get back? Sometimes all it takes to boost your confidence is to acknowledge that you're not doing what you want because you're *scared.*

And while you're at it, acknowledge that it's okay to be afraid of doing it, because we all are. We're *all* scared of abandoning the safe harbor of our lives to head into the open sea. But we do it anyway because *life's better that way.*

As a friend once told me: "You don't want to be a waste of skin, do you?"

Strategies for Building Belief

Beliefs are learned. We get them from parents, from teachers, from social groups, from colleagues, and from past experiences. Once we start to believe them, they become self-fulfilling prophecies and we find more and more support for them simply because we stop acting and thinking in ways contrary to them. The result is that we start thinking that the current way of doing things is the *only* way, and it gets hard—sometimes really hard—to see things differently.

The upside, though, is that we learned all these beliefs, and we can unlearn them. All it takes is a little persistence. Still not sure you can do it? Let's look at some ways to build belief—to boost your faith that you really can take time off and live to tell the tale physically, emotionally *and* financially.

The Guarantee

Ask yourself this question: If you knew, without a doubt, that you could not fail in your sabbatical—that the money, the job, the kids, the house would all work out just right, what would you do? Would there be anything left holding you back? Be honest. If you were *guaranteed* that your hiatus would be wildly successful, what would stop you from going? If the answer is "nothing", then the only reason you're not going is because you're scared that it *won't* work out.

It will.

Find the Worst-Case Scenario

Ask yourself this question: *What's the worst-case scenario, short of injury or death, that could happen if I do this?*

Calculate how much money you could lose. Now ask yourself: can I live with that? Keeping in mind that the worst-case scenario is highly unlikely, could I live with it if it happened? Are the benefits that I've imagined worth it?

Now, take it a step further: come up with a compelling argument of why the worst-case scenario would be *good*. How could it help? How could it be the best thing that ever happened to you?

Your knee-jerk response to this exercise will be to discount it. Don't. Stick it out, and force yourself to make a positive argument for the worst-case scenario. You'll find it remarkably freeing.

Ask "What's So Special?"

Ask around—you'll find someone who's taken time away. What's so special about them? If you're truly honest, you'll likely discover that they're probably not much different from you. They may have specialized skills, but so do you—and that's not a prerequisite for time off. As a matter of fact, you probably need your specialized skills more to stay home than you do to leave.

So if they're no different than you, what's the hold up? If they can do it, why can't you?

Take Action

Perhaps the best thing you can do to squash the fears that may be brewing inside you is to get started.

Most worries in life never come to pass. We worry constantly about things that we can't change, things that we can change (but don't), things that will never happen, and things that have *already* happened. Your sabbatical plans are no different. The majority of the things you worry about in planning your time away will never come to pass.

The best way to prove that is to start moving forward. Take action. Start the steps you'll find in this book that will move you toward your dream year, and watch as problems and challenges resolve themselves simply through the momentum of continuing to pursue your desire.

Ask "What if It's Not True?"

For every single mental barrier to your hiatus, ask yourself, "What if it's not true?" Think you need to quit your job to take time off? *What if it's not true?* Think you can't collect a salary while you're on sabbatical? *What if it's not true?*

Don't believe your beliefs. Start to nurture a healthy curiosity about whether what you and others believe is really accurate. You'll be surprised at what you discover.

Eliminate Can't

Make a point of eliminating words like *can't* and *impossible* from your vocabulary. They don't serve you. I'm not being new-agey; the words really don't add value, and occasionally (like when you're considering the idea of sabbatical) they close your mind too quickly to possibilities that might bring some real value to your life. Eliminating *can't* from your mental and verbal diet allows you to consider things more carefully before you discard them.

Generate Solutions: What if You Had To?

Belief is closely tied to the concept of *how*. Sometimes, we need to know *how* we're going to do something in order to believe that we can. Having a set of possible solutions instantly makes a problem appear much more solvable.

A classic self-help question to include here would be, "What if you only had one day/week/month/year to live? How would you spend your remaining time?" While this is helpful food for thought for generating ideas of *what* to do on sabbatical, it doesn't really do the job of generating ideas and solutions for *how* to do it.

Let's take it up a notch. This one is hard on the heart, but great for generating solutions. Think of your most cherished loved one—a spouse, child, or dear family member or friend. Now ask yourself this question:

If the only way I could save a loved one's life was to take six months off, how would I do it?

What you'll discover first is that you'll immediately abandon all concept of *can't*. Your immediate response will be, "I'll take six months off. Quit. Take sick leave. Whatever." So much for can't. Now take it a step further. What if, in order to save that person's life, you had to take six months off *without damaging your business or career?* Think it through. Remember that there's a life at stake here - you can't cop out. You'll be surprised at the creative ideas you'll come up with simply because you *have* to.

 C3

Don't underestimate *belief*. It's the cornerstone for everything in this book. Even something you desire powerfully will never come to pass unless you believe it can.

Remember that thousands and thousands of people have done this before, and many of them faced serious obstacles to do it. Don't be fooled into thinking that they had an advantage that you don't.

If you can buy and read this book, you can escape. Believe it.

THE THIRD SECRET: VISION

Go before you go.

Everything you can imagine is real.

-Pablo Picasso (1881 - 1973)

I N THE 1960'S, RESEARCHERS asked three separate groups to play basketball. In truth, it wasn't *really* basketball; they asked the participants to stand at the foul line and shoot hoops, one after the other, and the researchers kept score.

After the initial benchmarking, the three groups each received different sets of instructions. Group one practiced free throws on the court. Group two, the control, had no additional skills training or practice. Group three had no further time on the court, but the participants completed a series of mental envisioning exercises where they imagined themselves on the court, going through the process of shooting successful foul shots.

At the end of the study, each group's abilities were retested on the court. The control group—the ones with no additional physical *or* mental training—showed no improvement. As you might expect, the group with additional skills practice improved (by 24%, to be precise). The big surprise? The group whose only training was *imagining* themselves shooting successful foul shots improved by 23%—virtually the same amount as the group who trained physically![9]

How can this be? How can practicing in your mind be as effective as practicing "for real"? The explanation is that the subconscious mind cannot tell the difference between what is real, and what is vividly imagined. So much so, that we can improve in physical and mental skills simply by imagining ourselves performing the skills successfully. A clear mental *vision* of what it is we wish to successfully do is in itself a form of doing—it moves us along the learning curve without actually doing what it is we need to learn. It turns out that doing something "for real" has less to do with the physical world than it does our mental one.

Vision is the ability to clearly create a mental picture of your sabbatical. It requires no special skills—just the willingness to take a few minutes here and there to let your mind wander.

To create a vision of your hiatus, you need to imagine your time away in every detail possible. Imagine packing—what will you take? What will you leave? Imagine traveling to the airport and getting on the plane—who will take you? How long will the flight be?

Envision yourself on your sabbatical—the people, the culture, the food, the language. Where will you live? What will your days be like?

If your first response to these questions was, "How am I supposed to know what my sabbatical's going to be like? I haven't even *gone* yet?", then let's be more clear. This is about painting the clearest mental picture you can of your time away *as you would like it to be*. The purpose here is to take your powerful desire, suspend your disbelief, and *imagine*.

Let your imagination go. Don't limit your vision by where you are right now—your circumstances and mindset will be different when you leave—just enjoy conjuring up a vision of your perfect sabbatical. When your brain jumps in and says, "Well, nice vision, but too bad you'll never have the cash," push that out of your mind. Learn to eliminate negative thoughts from your vision.

If you're skeptical—come on, I know you are—here are some very practical, non-imaginative reasons for building your vision.

Why You Need Vision

It Enhances Desire

The clearer your vision of your time away, the more you'll start to want it. As your mental picture becomes clearer and clearer, your brain will start to drool in anticipation. The more you allow yourself to dream—which is really all vision is—the more excitement you'll start to feel.

Researchers have long believed that the subconscious mind can't tell the difference between something real and something clearly imagined. Skeptical? Think about your most vivid dream or nightmare. Remember how you felt when you were jolted awake in the middle of the night—sweating in fear or laughing with joy? Those experiences seem unbelievably real. Yet they *never happened.*

A clear mental picture will make what you want more concrete, and as a result, more desireable.

It Builds Belief

A highly realistic vision is remarkably similar to the real thing—brain researchers, athletes, coaches and mental health experts have known this for years. Many, many top athletes use an envisioning process to picture themselves in a competition before it happens. Like the basketball study, the evidence to support the effectiveness of this process is well-documented.

Unlike the athlete who's competed many times in their sport, however, you've likely never taken six months off to learn Swahili. What envisioning gives you is what an athlete already has—the belief that you can actually do this.

It Helps You Plan

The clearer your vision gets, the easier it gets to plan. As your mental image becomes clearer, you'll start to take note of little details that will help with your preparation. For example:

You walk into the romantically-lit piazza and sit at a small table set with fresh cut flowers. Your spouse looks amazing, the night air is the perfect temperature. A waiter approaches and welcomes you in Italian...

...wait a minute! Italian? I better pick up an Italian-English diction-ary before I go...

...and you respond with a phrase from your handy dictionary.

Learn to be a daydreamer. It's where the most vivid, compelling and exciting visions come from, and where the tiny details spring forth that help make your time away run that much more smoothly.

It Helps You Get Exactly What You Want

Your sabbatical vision is unique to you. Everyone has their own motivation for wanting to get away, and their own mental picture of what their escape will be like.

The challenge for many people is to get the mental picture to align with the real thing—that's where vision is a big help. Your clear envi-sioning of your sabbatical is a way of clarifying exactly what you want. As you start to develop a clear image of your time away, you'll naturally start to move toward things that meet that image, and also to attract things to you that are a match for your mental picture.

While each of the four secrets has its own role in helping your exit plan, *Vision* also plays a special role in ensuring that your time away is as good, or better, than you imagine.

Let me clarify: this is very practical. Consider the difference be-tween these two people:

Bob wants to take a break from work. "Anywhere's fine, as long as it's not here," is his standard story. When asked what he'd like to do, Bob's reply is usually, "Anything, as long as it's not work."

Contrast Bob with Sally. She wants to go on sabbatical, too, but she's spent a lot of time envisioning her time off—how long, where to go, what she'd like to do. Even what it'll *feel* like. She's even taken the time to write down her vision for her sabbatical, part of which looks something like this:

I'm going to take six months off, starting two years from now. I'll find a small home I can rent in the tropics—preferably someplace where they speak Spanish. I'll do volunteer work for an environmental organization while I'm there.

When asked about her plans, it's easy for Sally to say, "I want to do some volunteer environmental work in the tropics—ideally somewhere Spanish speaking."

The difference in attitude and focus is obvious, but what does that mean in terms of practical trip planning? It means Sally is going to find almost exactly what she wants. I can almost guarantee it. Why? *Because your best sabbatical opportunities will come from a personal contact, or someone they know.*

Accomplished job-seekers know that the best jobs come from contacts in their network. They know that the best way to find an opportunity is through friends, family, and friends of friends and family, and so on. Building a perfect sabbatical—find a great place to go, something amazing to do, and somewhere to stay, to list just a few components—is a networking job.

Don't worry—this isn't about sales. This kind of networking is simply talking about your passion! It's just about telling your story so people can help. And believe me, people love to help. We'll look at this in depth later, but for now, understand that achieving clarity about what you want from your time away makes it easy for people to help. In the example above, Bob's not going to get much help because no one knows *how* to help him. Sally, however, is going to discover that her colleague's cousin has a home in the environmentalist Mecca of Costa Rica, and desperately needs someone to house-sit for her.

Why is Sally going to find the perfect opportunity? Because she has a clear *vision*.

It Prepares You

Since your subconscious mind can't tell the difference between reality and imagination, what does that say about your sabbatical preparations? Envisioning your sabbatical will actually improve your ability to deal with pitfalls and handle the initial emotional ups and downs *before you go.*

C3

The secret to effective, enjoyable envisioning lies in one simple habit: allowing yourself the mental freedom to dream without criticism. We're all born with the natural ability to imagine—look at any child if you need proof—some of us just haven't done it in a while.

Try to remember that vision is not a "how", it's a "what". If you can free your mind from *how* you're going to accomplish the vision, you'll develop the habit of dreaming freely of *what can be*, as opposed to *why it can't*.

Once you crack that code, you're only one step away from success: building the momentum to make it all happen in the world outside your mind.

And with that in mind, it's time for the next step.

THE FOURTH SECRET: COMMITMENT

Create the point of no return.

Unless commitment is made, there are only promises and hopes... but no plans.

-Peter Drucker (1909 - 2005)

MY HOMETOWN SITS ON a beautiful, wide stretch of slow-moving river. Just a few minutes boat ride from the town pier, a sheer cliff face slides into the water, and continues down into the dark depths.

These cliffs, dubbed "the diving rocks" continue to be a destination for the adventurous youth of the area. (Or certain adults who refuse to grow up. Ahem.) For all of us, it was a rite of passage.

I'll always remember the first time. It requires some guts to make the jump. Even standing at the edge looking over is a little nerve-wracking, and many a run to the edge has been aborted at the last minute. But after all the cajoling, courage bolstering, strutting and backslapping that lead up to the jump are finished, there is a single step that is the most crucial. It's the *last* one. The step that takes you past the point of no return.

At any previous point, you can stop, retrace your steps and start over. Or even bail out altogether. But the one step that takes you over the edge carries a distinct feeling of "no turning back". Once you take that step, you give in to gravity and turning back is simply not an option.

The life you lead right now has a powerful gravitational pull of its own. Desire, belief and vision are all powerful forces that increase your ability and drive to get away, but inevitably the comfort and security of your life tend to pull you back toward status quo. That security is an opposing force, and not to be underestimated.

To escape the gravitational pull of *normal*, we need a fourth secret: *commitment*.

In the end, the real difference between the people who get what they truly want and the people who don't is commitment—the determination to move relentlessly toward a desire. All the desire, confidence and vision in the world won't get you to the African savannah if you aren't prepared to commit to going.

Now if this seems like a big deal, don't worry. This is about commitment made easy. Taking time away requires some guts, but you don't need to climb Everest without supplemental oxygen to demonstrate your commitment. (Unless, of course, that's your sabbatical plan.)

Commitment for our purposes here is about small steps that create:

1. Momentum towards your goal
2. Increasing levels of "investment" that make it difficult to *not* pursue your goal

Confused? Let's look at a related example. One of the toughest things for most people to deal with in getting away from it all is their work situation. (It's tough enough that there's a whole chapter coming up on it.) For career folks, it's not just the money. They've got a lot of *time* invested in their work. It may have taken years to reach their present position in the organization—they don't want to blow it all by taking six months off in Bora Bora. And what about retirement plans? Stock options? Bonuses? Those are all investments of one type or another, and they motivate you to *stay where you are*. In other words, they're a *commitment* that's already been made to your current life.

Let's look at an *Escape 101* definition for *commitment*:

Commitment: *an investment which, if not followed through on, generates a perceived emotional, mental or physical loss or pain.*

What does this say? It says that commitment is not just willpower or strength of character—that's called *drive*, and we all have it in varying amounts. Commitment contains more than drive. Commitment contains within it *our perception of the consequences of not following through.*

The four types of commitment that follow are about slowly changing the balance of comfort in your life. The objective is to gradually shift your thinking over time, so that the perceived consequences of not getting away outweigh the benefits of staying. In other words, your objective is to make it psychologically easier to leave than it is to stay.

It's been said that human beings only operate on two principles: pleasure and pain. That theory suggests that everything we do—every decision and action—is based on increasing pleasure, or avoiding pain. The secret of committing to your sabbatical plans in this context is simple: commitment is about making it more painful to *not* go. Or, if you prefer the opposite, commitment is about making it more pleasurable to leave than to stay.

The truth, however, is that most of us can't simply summon up a batch of commitment at will. It's not a *decision*. You can decide to take a year off, but that decision will only bear fruit if it's accompanied by commitment. That commitment is created by taking *action*.

More accurately put, commitment isn't one action, it's many. It takes time to build new habits, and for most people, change is a dish best served slowly. New Year's resolution-type decisions to lose weight, join a gym, become a new person, or spend less are seldom effective.

For best results, the action steps that build commitment to your sabbatical should be small and sustainable. Sure, you can cut all your spending and save like crazy—it's been done many, many times—but not everyone can sustain a monastic lifestyle for an extended period of time.

Here are the four types of commitment that will not only help make your sabbatical plans come to fruition, but they'll actually make it *easier* on you. And with enough commitment, eventually you'll find it really does become easier to leave than it is to stay.

We all place a different level of importance on each of these types of commitment. As you read through each one, try to get a feel for the level of impact that the commitment will have on you.

Financial

Financial commitment is a powerful motivator. In fact, financial commitment is pretty much a prerequisite for most sabbaticals—unless you have extensive savings or are independently wealthy, you'll need some level of financial commitment to make your time away happen.

The chapter on money will give you specific techniques for dealing with the financial end of things, but for now, here are some examples of financial commitments:

Savings. You'll need some cash for this, naturally. Starting a savings plan creates a powerful commitment to your sabbatical.

Trip Expenditures. Committing financially isn't limited to saving. Money spent in advance can be far more powerful. Non-refundable plane tickets and deposits are particularly strong motivators. If you can't get the money *back*, you'll simply have to go on sabbatical to get your money's *worth*.

Financial Sacrifice. Though not always required, cutting your budget and "going without" generates increased commitment to the cause. If you give up the new addition to your home or cancel your summer vacation in order to save for your time away, that time away immediately becomes more important because you've sacrificed to make it happen.

Social

Social commitment is created by telling friends, family and colleagues that you are indeed leaving. While not a motivator for everyone, telling someone you're going to do something is a powerful force for some. Not losing face, being true to your word—if these are important concepts in your life, then social commitment will serve you well on the path to your sabbatical.

Once you've made your decision, tell your friends and family, and then remember the commitment you've made. Relish the joy of being a person of integrity. Feel the pain of what it would be like to *not* follow through. Cultivate a sense of reliability. Consider yourself a role model for responsibility, and feel the pressure.

And remember: most people secretly want to do what you're doing. If it helps you to commit, consider the bragging rights you'll be earning on your hike through the Himalayas.

Logistical

There are many decisions to be made in planning for your trip, but some are particularly important for their practical role in increasing your commitment. Logistical commitments are actions that make it harder to *not* go. They simply make it awkward or difficult to not follow through. Some examples:

Rent your home. If you own your own home, and decide to rent it out for extra money while you're away, then you've created a logistical commitment: you no longer have a place to live.

Quit your job. Once the other shoe drops at work, it may be difficult to reverse the decision. Someone will need to be hired, at least temporarily, to replace you, so there's no going back.

Hire someone to run your business. If you promote or hire someone to operate your business in your absence, you've just taken a big step down the sabbatical road. You've officially replaced yourself, so now what? You might as well get going—someone else is running the show, now.

Book the time. In a world where the calendar is king, and you can find a clock just about anywhere you look (except Las Vegas), scheduling can work to your advantage. If you use a calendar system of any type, just book the time off. That's it. It's a ten-second task, but it's remarkably effective. Not only does it work wonders for getting your brain in sabbatical gear, but it serves a real practical purpose as your exodus date approaches: it keeps the time sacred. It's amazing how easily a sabbatical can be delayed or derailed by an "open" calendar.

Commit by locking in the time now.

Of course, *all* these decisions are reversible, or could be re-engineered so that you don't *have* to leave, but the point is that each one makes it a little harder to stay, and a little easier to go.

Mental/Emotional

To some extent all of these commitments are emotional ones. They all are designed to make you feel the pain of not following through. However, there are specific emotional triggers that can be used as leverage in your quest to get away. These may not all resonate with you, but if you find one that does, latch onto it tightly. It'll serve you well.

Goal setting. Goals tend to be a binary thing. They either work for people, or they don't. The people for whom goals are an effective emotional tool tend to be people motivated by the challenge of achieving them. Once they set a goal, they'll go after it like a tiger simply because it's a goal.

If you're motivated by the challenge, or the thrill of the chase, you might find goal setting is a powerful way to increase your commitment. If you've never set goals, there are no shortage of books, courses, audio programs and coaches out there to help you do it.

Values and personality. If work-life balance, or your health, or your relationships are important to you, then *not* taking your sabbatical is going to cause you some pain. Similarly, if the thought of *failure* (not going) or being *wrong* (claiming you can take a sabbatical, then not being able to) make you feel uncomfortable, then you've found another commitment trigger. Latch on to it.

CB

Of the four secrets, commitment is the most tangible and action-oriented. It's the first real step in moving your plans from the relative safety of your thoughts, to the real world where the sabbatical rubber meets the road. It's a crucial step—fail to commit in real-world terms, and your hiatus may remain just out of reach, relegated to permanent dream status.

The secret to commitment is to "commit early, commit often". Try to make your first commitments as soon as possible. Financial commitment is often the most important and most effective, and in these times of internet banking, an automated monthly withdrawal can be implemented in just a few minutes.

How the Four Secrets Interact

The sequencing of the four secrets is no accident. If you don't *want* to take time away (Desire) then there's not much point in trying to convince yourself that you can do it (Belief). There's a natural progression at work.

Each of the four secrets—Desire, Belief, Vision and Commitment—stands alone as its own powerful force in bringing your time away to fruition. Any one of those forces can take you from cubicle dreamer to world traveler.

Things really start to happen, though, when the four secrets come together. Desire fuels an increasingly vivid Vision of your time away. That growing Vision empowers a Belief, and leads to action in the form of Commitment. Commitment, in turn creates more Desire, and the cycle starts again, with the four combining in new and recurring patterns that propel you forward toward the year of your dreams.

The synergy of each of the four secrets creates something far greater than the sum of the parts. While you may naturally be more attracted to (or skilled at) one or two of the secrets, take the time to master them all, and enjoy the incredible sensation of creating your life exactly the way *you* want it.

CB

The next section of *Escape 101* focuses on the more tangible aspects of escaping—leaving jobs and businesses, finding opportunities and dealing with finances. You may have found it tempting to skim through the first part of the book, ready to dive into these practical aspects of your sabbatical. While these real-world tips and tools are important in their own right, it's critical to remember that these things are secondary to the four secrets. These logistical aspects of getting away are simply the practical steps necessary to execute the vision you create through the use of the four secrets.

If you haven't got a handle on the four secrets—if you haven't yet taken the time to embrace them and put them to work for you—give them their due. While taking a sabbatical without them is possible, you may find it more difficult, stressful, and expensive than just staying put.

If you're well prepared with desire, belief, vision and commitment, then it's time to get into preparations in the *physical*, as opposed to the mental, world.

The most profound difference you'll notice as you leave behind your inner world, and start to move into the realm of execution is that things may suddenly *seem* harder. Don't be fooled. They aren't. They just appear that way.

It *is* relatively easy to dream up a perfect sabbatical; most of us spend at least some time imagining our perfect day, week, or year. And things can fall apart in bringing that vision to fruition. The roadblocks and challenges we face can threaten our confidence, and without persistence, can derail our plans. The bold plans we made to negotiate six months off may suddenly seem foolish when we arrive at the office the next day. What seems like easy financial planning one month may seem impossible when unexpected bills arrive the next. Remember, though, these roadblocks are mainly *mental* challenges.

How can you cope with these setbacks? How do you keep the momentum of your "inner sabbatical" going when your "outer sabbatical" is threatened?

The trick is to return to the four secrets. Remember that escape really is an inside job—the only difference between those who do and those who don't is mindset. Use the four secrets as touchstones for your sabbatical. There will be setbacks and surprises—expect them, and stay the course. Return to your vision every time, and you *will* find your dream hiatus. Guaranteed.

PART 2: Planning It

Make no little plans; they have no magic to stir men's blood...Make big plans, aim high in hope and work.

- Daniel H. Burnham (1846 - 1912)

BIG ROCKS: THE PRINCIPLE OF ESCAPE PLANNING

I N HIS BOOK *Big Rocks: Balancing Life & Work*, Dr. Gary F. Russel tells the story of Jack Bedford, an overworked corporate employee who's slowly losing the time management war. When he changes jobs to find some relief, he instead finds more of the same. As his life slowly deteriorates, it looks like Jack's got himself an express ticket to a nervous breakdown.

A chance meeting with a stranger at a soccer game leads Jack to a lecture on something called "Big Rocks". At the session, Jack learns the value in planning the big things—health, relationships, education, etc.— before the small things like dry cleaning and shopping.

The idea of "Big Rocks" has been around for many years, and has been used as a practical demonstration in many a time management workshop using a large jar, some rocks and a pile of sand. The only way to get everything into the jar is to put the big rocks in first, and then allow the sand to fit around them; try the opposite, and the stuff simply won't fit. The big rocks represent the truly important things in life; fail to deal with them first, and you'll likely fail to deal with them at *all*.

But I'm trying to get away from time management, you say? Get away you shall, but the big rocks principle is an apt one for planning your escape. The devil, as it turns out, is most certainly in the details. In fact, getting caught up in the details is a sure way to spook yourself off the sabbatical train before it even leaves the station. Successful sabbatical planning requires a big rocks approach.

This section is about tackling the big rocks. Things like money, careers, businesses and children. The big, scary immovable boulders that take sabbaticals off the rails at the planning stage (which, you'll recall, is why we don't start with planning).

Imagine the really big things in your sabbatical planning as large boulders at the top of a hill. They're big, they're heavy, and they're immobile. They haven't shifted an inch in a *long* time.

Anything that big takes a little energy to get moving. Once you get them going though, those big rocks roll downhill with incredible speed. Once you start them, you don't have to push them any more. They just keep on rolling.

And the details? Surprisingly, most details aren't that...*detailed*. Many turn out to be unimportant or irrelevant, and the ones that are important are usually pretty easy to take care of. Once your big mental rocks get moving, they tend to just roll right over the little stuff along the way.

How Long?

Your time away can be as long as you choose—after all, it's *your* sabbatical. However, you'll find that a two week vacation—even if you leave your cell phone behind—is not going to give you the same experience as something a little longer.

My experience is that six months to a year is a common range for escape seekers. Six months is long enough to fully decompress from work and other "real life" scenarios, but still within the range of affordability. I would consider three months as the absolute minimum, but again, it's up to you.

It's not that you can't have a mind-blowing, brain-expanding, perspective-creating epiphany in a few days at Club Med. It's just that more often than not, you *won't*.

Vacation and sabbatical are not the same. You need time to decompress. Time to slough off the cares of home. It can take weeks just to adjust to not being responsible for work and other projects from your home life. It's common for people to report taking more than a month just to get used to not making stressful work decisions. If you've been busy in the rat race—even doing something you absolutely love—you're going to need to learn a new way of looking at things. Slowing your pace, and doing it without anxiety, is a skill. It might not be one that you have. Yet.

Where?

While your sabbatical can be anywhere you choose, I'd recommend you give some thought to doing more than kicking around the house. Taking a sabbatical has become almost synonymous with travel, but that's not the point. The point is that staying in familiar surroundings has a way of keeping you in familiar patterns of thinking and behavior. And if you don't change those, what's really changed?

The gift of a sabbatical is perspective. There are many, many benefits, but the real treasure is the new set of eyes from which you get to see yourself and your life. It's difficult to gain that perspective without leaving home.

Even if you want to take time off from work to write a book, learn to paint, or train for the Olympics—arguably all things you could do without moving to a new city or country—consider the option of doing it somewhere besides where you are right now. You won't regret it.

How Long from Right Now?

Let's assume for the moment you know where you'd like to go, and how long you'd like to go for. When can you leave?

There's certainly no single right answer for this, but before you start running the numbers on saving accounts, stock portfolios, and airline prices to find your perfect exit date, consider that there just might not be a right answer.

In *The 4-Hour Workweek*, serial vagabond Timothy Ferriss challenges status quo thinking, urging readers to reconsider everything about traditional work structures and rules. In the section on *Rules that Change the Rules*, he declares, "The Timing is Never Right":

> "For all of the most important things, the timing always sucks. Waiting for a good time to quit your job? The stars will never align and the traffic lights of life will never all be green at the same time. The universe doesn't conspire against you, but it doesn't go out of its way to line up all the pins, either. Conditions are never perfect. "Someday" is a disease that will take

*your dreams to the grave with you. Pro and con lists are just as bad. If it's
important to you and you want to do it "eventually", just do it and correct
course along the way."[10]*

So what's the takeaway? *Don't wait.* Time is certainly your ally in
planning, particularly on the financial side, but don't be fooled into
waiting for the right timing. Never, ever wait.

It's also important to keep in mind that *you will use whatever time you
give yourself.* If you decide it'll take five years to get prepared for your
hiatus, it'll take five years. If you give yourself five months, it'll take that
long too. My suggestion? Pick a time you're comfortable with, then
slash about 25-50% of it and recalibrate accordingly. Chances are you'll
hit your target, and if it takes a bit longer, you won't have lost anything.
Push yourself a little on this. You won't regret it.

For the moment, if you haven't got a specific duration and destination in time, accept that those things will fall into place as you begin
your plan. And to get started with that plan, it's time to put your
shoulder against one of the biggest rocks of all: *money*.

FIGURING OUT THE MONEY

Lack of money is no obstacle. Lack of an idea is an obstacle.

-Ken Hakuta

An unhurried sense of time is in itself a form of wealth.

-Bonnie Friedman
The New York Times

SIX NEW PESOS. It was the last of our money—a little over a buck. We'd been traveling through Central America, and now, having made our way back up the east coast to Mexico's Yucatan Peninsula, we were low on cash, to put it mildly.

Back then, the term "Mayan Riviera" wasn't common. Cancun was booming, but we were south of there so our low cash situation wasn't really a problem. We'd pitched our tent in a campsite in Playa del Carmen, a sleepy beach town on the mainland just a short ferry ride from the island of Cozumel where we planned to catch our flight home.

We'd used the last of our cash over the weekend, but life was cheap in Playa del Carmen. We'd pre-paid a few nights camping when we arrived, so we had a place to stay for the weekend, and on Monday we planned to hit the bank and get a cash advance on our credit card to give us the money to get to Cozumel, have a couple of meals, pay our airport taxes and depart. No big deal—a hundred bucks would be lots.

Monday morning we spent our last dollar on banana bread for breakfast, and casually wandered over to the bank to grab some cash and book a ferry to the island. It was another beautiful sunny morning, and we were enjoying the day and the thought of getting home. All was right with the world.

We found a clerk inside the bank, and told him we needed a cash advance on our credit card. "*No hay problema, señor,*" he responded cheerfully. No surprise—we'd done this a few times.

I pulled my credit card out of my shorts, and with a horrible sinking feeling, realized that *it had gone through the wash*. And the dryer. It was now bent, and while somewhat legible, it was a shadow of its former self.

The card was refused. It was also too mangled to use in a bank machine. None of the hotels would help. All the banks turned us away. We were thousands of miles from home, with absolutely no money, no food, and nowhere to stay.

I felt like I was going to throw up. What were we going to do? We needed to be at an airport in a few hours, and we didn't have the money to *eat*, never mind pay our ferry tickets and departure taxes.

Thank goodness for low budget travel—it really does connect you to people. When we reached the campsite, another backpacker took one look at us and asked, "Are you okay?" We told our story to this perfect stranger, who handed us $100, and said, "Here's my address. Send me the cash when you get home."

Not long after, we were on a plane home, overwhelmed by the generosity of strangers, and stunned by our own stupidity and poor financial planning.

❧

Money is the first step in the planning section for good reason. It's important stuff—don't kid yourself. Although you don't need a lot of it to get away, money will make your sabbatical easier. And time and money are good companions; the more time you give yourself to plan the money side of your getaway, the easier things will be. This makes it important to get started as early as possible.

Mainly, though, money is first because it's the single biggest mental roadblock to getting away. It's the biggest of the big rocks, and likely the first thing that comes to mind when you consider the logistics of taking extended time off. Sadly, for many people it's also the *last* thing that comes to mind—they never get past the money stage at all. Nearly every fear and mental obstacle related to your plans for an extended hiatus can be traced back to money. To put this to the test, think of something that's worrying you regarding your sabbatical, or preventing you from taking action. Now ask yourself, "could this be solved if I had a million dollars?" If the answer is yes, then your concern is financial. Try this on a few of your problems, and you'll discover money is likely a big hairy deal when it comes to sabbatical planning.

Does this mean that you need a million extra dollars to get away? Of course not. It means that it's important to recognize money as a big player in exiting the rat race, and that you'll need a system for dealing with it.

What follows are five steps to dealing with the financial side of your sabbatical. Depending on your situation, some of them may be optional for you. Chances are, though, you're thinking, "How can I afford this?" You can—read on.

Consider all the steps with an open mind. If you follow all five, you can virtually guarantee the following:

- A sabbatical free of financial worry and strain
- Untouched savings and retirement plans
- Stable home finances

And you might also find the following unexpected financial windfalls:

- A business that grows in your absence
- Increased income
- New sources of income

Dealing with the financial side of your sabbatical requires nothing more than a few minutes, and a system. This is that system.

Financial Escape Step #1: Open Your Mind/Dispel Myths

The big difference between people who find it easy to deal with the financial side of time off, and those who struggle with it is not income, it's mindset. *How you think about money, not how much you have, will be the single biggest factor in your ability to escape your normal life.*

The first step to successful sabbatical finances is to change the way you think about the sabbatical-money relationship. When you think about taking extended time away from work or business, do you think of living in poverty? Of sacrificing your life savings? Of driving your business into the ground? Of losing a hard-earned position with your company? Most of us would be lying if we didn't admit to having these fears when we consider planning a long absence from our regular life. In fact, having these fears helps us ensure that we're careful in planning our time away. Our fears serve the valuable purpose of identifying *what we feel strongly about.* The crossover point occurs when those fears are no longer an indicator of something important to us, but become an inhibitor of action; when they freeze us in place, they've passed the point of usefulness.

Enjoying a sabbatical free of financial worry starts with dispelling the myths of sabbatical finances, and planting new beliefs about what's really required to escape and stay solvent. If the following beliefs aren't new to you, congratulations—you're on the road to your dream year. If they are new, or perhaps seem outrageous, try "suspending your disbelief" long enough to *consider* the possibility that they just might be true. You don't need to change your mind right now. Just allow yourself the luxury of considering what follows. Tell yourself you'll pretend it's true for a few minutes, and then you can go back to your old way of thinking if you like. And regardless, it won't cost you anything to be open-minded for a few pages.

You Don't Need to Be Rich

People from every socio-economic category take time off. The poor, the middle class and the ultra-rich all take sabbaticals. And conversely, even more poor, middle class and ultra-rich people also continue to *not* take sabbaticals, too. Why? *Because income level is not a good predictor of your ability to take a sabbatical.* In fact, for many people there's a negative correlation—the higher their income, the more they have to lose, and the more they perceive extended time off as risky.

Regardless of your income right now, you can find a way to make your time away happen. I've met people from all walks of life, in every conceivable financial situation who have simply dropped out of life for a year. From monk-poor to Trump-rich, they're just making it happen.

If money is a significant roadblock for you, start with baby steps. Allow yourself to admit that yes, you *could* do it if you wanted to. You don't have to commit—just begin by acknowledging that regardless of money, you *could*.

You're Richer Than You Think You Are

If you live in the First World—which, if you're reading this book, you likely do—you probably have more money than you think you do.

When asked to squeeze a little more out of their budget, the knee-jerk reaction for most people, "I can't". However, if you closely examine most spending habits in detail, you find that a great deal of money flows to luxuries and unnecessary expenses.

I don't believe in budgets or in tightening the belt. If you're worried that this is one of those "make your own lunch to save a buck" books, you can rest easy. This isn't an exercise in squeezing every latte out of your coffee budget—it's a simple acknowledgment that you likely have some flexibility in your finances.

You Don't Need to Spend Your Life Savings

If the first thing that springs to mind for you when contemplating a sabbatical is the loss of all the equity in your life—things like savings, retirement plans, stocks, bonds and real estate—then think again. *Your sabbatical will only be as expensive as you want it to be.* You control how much it costs. If you want to use your savings (more on this later) that's up to you. But if you think you *have* to cash in your stocks, think again.

It Doesn't Have to Cost a Lot

It doesn't have to cost *anything*, for that matter. Rewire your thinking on this. Sabbaticals can be cheap. Really cheap. Sabbatical math is different—the same rules don't apply. We'll talk more about this in Step

5—Finding The Right Sabbatical Opportunity, but for now, take my word that time away can be a heck of a lot cheaper than staying home.

The Benefits of Budget Travel

If your idea of a sabbatical is six months in five star hotels, don't let me stop you. I wouldn't mind that myself. However, if that's your idea of time away, but you can't *afford* it, you might consider some of the remarkable benefits of budget travel.

We've experienced the full spectrum of sabbatical experience, from homelessness to Hilton-ness, and while the big-budget experience has its own set of compelling features, the low-cost getaway is not to be missed.

Budget travel forces you into a whole new set of accommodation choices. Camping, hostels, guest houses and other forms of shared lodging become the norm, and while it may seem strange at first, the most dominant advantage is that you meet an enormous number of people. After years of escaping, the real memories we tend to return to are the people we've met, and very rarely have we met them from the climate controlled privacy of a hotel suite.

If you've never done it, it may seem strange, but why not try it? Mix up your time away. If you're older, don't worry—the hostels and campgrounds of the world are filled with people from a remarkable array of demographic groups.

Budget travel may also mean that you spend more time just *being*. With a larger budget, you tend to get a lot busier on sabbatical—shows, side trips and attractions start to fill up the days. If you don't have the money for opera tickets, you might just have to read a good book, walk with your spouse, or watch the sunset. Not as flashy as the opera, sure, but it's not as *loud*, either.

Budget travel leads you to more relationships, and more moments. Give it a try.

You Don't Have to Sacrifice Your Career

For those on the career track, there comes a point on the corporate ladder where the investment to date—the years spent working from entry-level mail room jobs to wherever you are now—is not just the experience and dues paid that helped you climb higher, but also the golden handcuffs that keep you from leaving. If you've been in one job for some time, or you've invested heavily in your career, fear not. You can do this without sacrificing your progress thus far.

"Career breaks" are now becoming far more commonplace. In fact, a survey by New York-based Catalyst shows 18% of Gen X'ers (born between 1964 and 1978) taking leaves and sabbaticals. That's almost one in five![11]

Not only is it more common, it's becoming increasingly acceptable in the workplace to take time away. Many progressive employers consider it a sign of initiative and drive. Others see travel as a way of building tolerance and interpersonal skills. Regardless of what your employer may think, you're not alone in your desire to get away.

You might also find that your time away can actually help your career. Sabbaticals have a tendency to be a form of intensive learning—you can learn new skills, acquire a language, and build wisdom in a shorter period of time then you might at home. Time away, particularly in a new culture, forces you to adapt to new situations in a way that you never would at home. These "soft skills" emerge in the workplace as improved decision-making, long-term thinking, and communication skills—all qualities that employers find valuable in today's market.

If you've denied yourself the opportunity to dream about taking a year off because of your commitment to your career, now is the time to open the door to the possibility. You might be pleasantly surprised.

You Can Come Back Financially Healthier

Sabbaticals are a great financial teacher. The process of saving, budgeting, spending wisely (and foolishly) is all part of learning more about money. Our last sabbatical enabled us to grow our businesses, develop passive income sources, *finally* learn to spend less than we earn, and pay ourselves first. These are the cornerstones of financial independence, and, ironically, *not* working was critical to mastering them.

You may also find that time away gives you new courage to do things you might never have done in your "regular" life: ask for a raise, switch jobs or careers, return to school, or start a business. These can all result in furthering your financial life in ways you might never have imagined. Who says you can't come back from your career break and get a job that pays twice as much? Or make twice as much at the same job? Taking the time to step away from your job gives you a whole new perspective that can't be acquired by getting up and *doing* the job day after day.

Your Business Can Thrive

If you're self-employed, or operate a business of any size, taking a sabbatical might well be one of the single best business decisions you ever make. In fact, it's so important that we've dedicated a whole chapter to it.

It's very easy, particularly in small companies, for business owners to feel that their business can't operate without them there. They feel that in order for things to be done right, they must do it themselves. It's a common scenario, but it's also one which is easily cured by taking time away.

Taking a sabbatical forces business owners to create *systems*—learnable, repeatable, consistent ways of doing business—that can be executed by someone else. Not only does this mean your business can make you money while you're away, it means it can continue to do so *after you return*. Taking a sabbatical may well be the permanent cure for the work overload that created the drive to get away in the first place!

Richer on the Road: An Example

If you're not convinced that sabbaticals can be cheap, or even profitable, here's some real data from our own experience.

Our last sabbatical lasted half a year. We did volunteer work with homeless kids in South America. In return for working part-time on the site, we had a nice cabin to stay in. We paid US$150 for food per month. In theory, that was all we needed, but we opted to also have a cell phone and internet access for another US$60 per month. Throw in some extra grub once in a while, and a few personal items, and you're still at US$250 per month in total.

We saved a small amount each month for four years to pay for our plane tickets. We rented our house before we left. That was just enough to cover mortgage, utilities, insurance, etc. In other words, we needed $250 a month to live comfortably. Period.

That's cheap. If you want to take six months off at those rates, you could do it on your credit card if you really wanted to. It's less than most people's monthly gasoline budget.

Taking a sabbatical can be cheap. It can be *free*. Just start by opening your mind to the possibility.

Financial Escape Step #2: Start Saving

The more you've got "tucked away" come sabbatical time, the more options you'll have, the less stress you'll have, and the more things you'll be able to do with your time. Although your time away doesn't have to be expensive, more money gives you more flexibility.

If you're cringing at the thought of trying to save, you may be surprised to find that it's not as difficult as you think. *Just about everything you need to do to save enough money for your sabbatical can be done in 30 minutes.* Yup. It's true. It's not a big deal. Thirty minutes of your time, then just get on with your life until your airport shuttle arrives. What could be easier?

It's important to note that this step is called *start* saving, not just "save". It's critical to just *start*. *The amount is not as important as the act.* Saving is commitment. Even a tiny amount builds confidence, and sets in motion all the other activities that make getting away possible.

Here are the key stages to your sabbatical savings plan:

Stage 1: Earn More

Even the good "savers" tend to miss out on this important first step when setting money aside. Before you do anything else, ask yourself this question: is there anyway I can earn more money first?

Why? First of all earning more money means you can put more aside than you might otherwise. Second—and this is the best part— earning more means you can put money aside *without changing your current spending habits*. If you can earn more, but tuck that extra away before it hits your wallet, you'll be able to spend as you do now, while still building your sabbatical fund. It's pain-free savings.

This step isn't essential to saving enough money, it simply allows you to save more money, more easily.

So how can you earn more? Here are just a few ideas:

- Ask for a raise—the easiest solution of all. You don't have to work harder, or cut your spending. Just ask, receive, and save the increase.

- If you work in a position with bonuses, find a way to perform better.
- Start a business—even a small home business can pay for your sabbatical.
- If you have a business, grow it.
- Get a higher-paying job.
- Get a second "sabbatical" job.
- Rent out part of your home.

The critical thing to remember is to move to the next stage right away. If you just got a hard-earned raise, you need to deal with that extra money before the mall does. This stage only works if you *save the increase*, as we'll do in Stage 2.

A Note On "Cashing Out"

One way to fund your time away is to liquidate some sort of equity you have in your life—sell your home or business, or cash in retirement plans, insurance, and other investments.

It's an easy and tempting way to quickly raise the capital you need to take time away, and it's been successfully done by many an escape artist. Don't let me stop you.

Consider, however, that it might be worth trying to do it without those things. By nature, we humans tend to rise to challenges. In the absence of a challenge, we tend to under-perform. If you know you can sell your home or cash in your investments to fund your time off, you're not likely to follow the steps outlined here. That's fine, but consider what happens in a year when you're back at work. Trust me, the time is going to fly by. Will you wish you'd kept your home? Maintained your investments?

Cashing out in order to take time away is fine. But it puts you in the position of not *having* to save or earn more, and that makes saving less likely to happen. Consider giving the steps in this chapter a shot. And while you're at it, consider making a commitment to continue paying into your retirement and other savings plans while you're gone. You'd be surprised at how easily you'll be able to do it if you have to.

If you're selling your assets to buy other escape-critical assets—another home, a sailboat, a motor home—then no problem. Other than market changes and depreciation, you should be able to recover most of your equity from these things.

If you're planning a sabbatical of a year or more, I'd recommend selling your personal vehicles. For six months or less, I'd keep them. In between six months and a year, it really depends on the car, insurance costs, and whether you have access to free storage.

Stage 2: Make It Automatic

Just about every financial planning book on earth includes this step. Having money automatically withdrawn from your bank account, or taken off your paycheck and transferred to some form of savings is perhaps the single greatest advance in personal wealth building since compound interest.

If you've done this before—for retirement plans, union dues, insurance payments, mortgages, car payments, automatic bill payments, etc.—then you'll know that once the money starts coming out, you adapt. Life goes on, you continue to put food on the table, and the payments are made without you doing anything. It's all automated, and before you know it, you've got a tidy little slush fund built up (or someone else does, if you're paying something off).

Happily, automatic savings eliminate the distasteful (and for the most part ineffective) task of creating a home budget in order to cut costs to pay for your sabbatical. *Saving for your sabbatical is not about cutting your costs; it's about changing the sequence in which you manage your money.* Automating your savings forces you to contribute to your sabbatical fund *first*.

It couldn't be easier to do. Just visit the bank, open a new savings account, and arrange a monthly transfer from your checking account. Done. If you bank online, you can probably do it all without getting up from your chair.

There are many options for exactly where to put the money—ask your banker, accountant or financial planner for advice. Just make sure that wherever money goes, it adheres to the next stage in the process.

Stage 3: Put it Out of Reach

As your fund starts to build, it's inevitable that a large expense will crop up—a new roof for your house, a medical expense, a new car, etc. Or you'll simply be tempted by the pile of money just sitting there screaming, "Home theatre!" When this happens (and it will), it'll be tempting to spend your hard-won sabbatical savings.

The solution to this is to ensure that your savings are being transferred to somewhere "out of reach". For example, you can put money into a savings account that isn't accessible by ATM, or online. The money's still there, but you have to physically go into the bank and withdraw cash. For many folks, that little extra step makes it that much *less* likely that they'll spend it.

Better yet, a term deposit or GIC will lock up the money so you *can't* get at it without penalty. This is even better. Put lump sums into GIC's with a term that ends just before your planned departure date. What could be more perfect?

When you head to that appointment you made with your banker in the previous stage, make sure you arrange to have your funds out of reach.

Sometimes it's wise to put your savings *and* your credit out of reach. While we're here, let's consider cutting up your credit cards. It's not my job to tell you how to spend your money, but consumer debt is a sabbatical killer. Making huge payments to credit cards during your time away will keep you hemorrhaging cash for the duration of your hiatus. If there's a chance that your monthly sabbatical savings are going to be offset by a corresponding increase in credit card balances, then you'll need to deal with this.

If you're like me and can't be trusted with credit cards, but still like to have them around in case of emergency, then take them out of your wallet and put them somewhere safe. I have one high-limit credit card in my sock drawer for big things, and one low-limit card in my wallet for small emergencies. That way I can buy plane tickets for our trips at home online, but not a $4000 home theatre when I'm at the mall. If you don't have a low limit card, you can create one simply by calling the company and changing your credit limit on an existing card.

You can also build a savings plan of sorts with credit cards, but only if they have no balance. If your cards are empty, for example, you can slowly build up a credit balance which you can draw from while you're away. Not ideal, but if cash on hand is too tempting for you, it beats not saving *anything*.

Stage 4: Stretch Yourself

Remember "You're richer than you think you are" from the beginning of this chapter? Challenge yourself to tap those riches. Make your automatic savings plan aggressive. Chances are you'll be just fine—you'll barely notice. And you can always change the amount if you absolutely have to.

Over time, increase the amount of your withdrawals as you adapt to the cash flow changes. Push yourself to save more. It'll save you from having to put yourself on a budget—the automatic savings will take care of that...well, automatically.

Financial Escape Step #3: Build a Sabbatical Income

(Note: This step is optional, but read on—you might just discover something interesting.)

One of the easiest ways to reduce the financial pressure of taking time away from work is to continue to earn money while you're gone. Depending on your financial situation, skills and career, this step is optional.

When you consider a sabbatical income, though, remember that you don't necessarily have to replace the entire income you have now. The finances of your sabbatical are entirely different from your regular life. Depending on where you are and what you're doing, the tiniest bit of extra money might buy you some peace of mind. Every little bit helps.

Here are a few options for maintaining some income during your sabbatical:

Take paid leave

It's not at all unheard of for people to be paid to take time off. No, really, it's true. Depending on your job, your industry, and exactly what you'll be doing on your sabbatical, you may be able to collect all, or a portion of your salary while you're gone. If your company isn't one of the approximately 5% of companies that officially offer paid sabbaticals, that shouldn't stop you from pursuing the idea anyway.[12]

The trick with paid leave is to make a case for it, and pitch it to the powers-that-be (your boss). We'll be discussing the whole topic of negotiating your time away in a later chapter, but for now, consider the possibility that you might not have to abandon your paycheck entirely.

Start a business

There's a whole upcoming chapter dedicated to leaving a business while maintaining its profitability. If you're a business owner, that chapter's for you.

If you don't currently run a business, or never have, it's worth thinking about. Technology has made small, portable businesses quite viable. You can run an internet business from anywhere on earth, and make a few bucks on the side. Or you can start a traditional business, and then hire someone to manage it in your absence.

Buy a Business/ Real Estate

If you don't have anything that can generate revenue for you while you're on sabbatical, don't let that stop you. You can buy income generating real estate, or a viable business that can generate cash flow for you during your time away.

While this may not be up your alley, the idea here is to open your mind to the possibility that there are other ways to earn a buck.

Freelance

Just as technology has changed the face of business, it's enabled thousands of people to earn a living as self-employed freelancers. Writers, graphic designers, computer programmers, bookkeepers and a multitude of other professions have become portable. In his book *The World is Flat*, Thomas J. Friedman describes the great changes that occurred during the tech bubble that now allow people to work from almost anywhere in the world. (As it happens, I'm writing this paragraph in rural Paraguay, staying in touch via internet on a cellular modem plugged into my laptop.)

> "...there was a massive investment in technology, especially in the bubble era, when hundreds of millions of dollars were invested in putting broadband connectivity around the world—undersea cables, all those things....They created a platform where intellectual work, intellectual capital, could be delivered from anywhere...this gave a whole new degree of freedom to the way we do work..."[13]

Travel writers abound these days, but even a personal blog (an internet journal) on your adventures can allow you to sell a few books via Amazon, or earn some advertising revenue. The systems are all there for you—it just takes a little time and desire. And on sabbatical, a few bucks can go a long way.

Seek Sponsors

> *"I basically just asked. I threw a dinner party where I told everyone what I was doing, and just asked for support. Everyone was very positive."*
>
> -A.C., Missionary

Many people take time off on the generosity of others, without feeling selfish, lazy, or opportunistic. Depending on what you're doing with your time away, you might consider approaching a church for funding, a business for equipment or supplies, or an individual for personal sponsorship.

Usually this type of sponsorship will require you to give something back, but it's remarkably little for what you get. You may have to send letters or emails to your sponsors to let them know what you're doing and how their money is being spent, or you might make a presentation when you return. It's easy, and the best part is that it's truly rewarding for both you *and* your sponsors.

The trick with sponsors is to find a benefit for them, or at minimum, a match with their values or interests. Most large companies have a charity of choice, and if it fits with your sabbatical plans, they can support you and meet their own mandate at the same time.

Move Your Job Somewhere Else

> *"I don't think we'll ever go home. Our kids will graduate from an international school somewhere. Why would we? We have everything we need here, and for the first time in our lives, we're saving money instead of spending it."*
>
> -Family of four, teaching in South America

While this book is more about *leaving* your job than moving it, sometimes a change is as good as a rest. Depending on your profession, you may be able to find work elsewhere, or arrange an official "work exchange". Or, as with freelancing, you can simply move your current job to a new location.

A Note On Sabbatical Incomes

If you're considering a sabbatical income, be aware that it will change the nature of your time away. If, for example, you negotiate to do a portion of your original job remotely—via email, internet or phone—you'll have more difficulty immersing yourself in the sabbatical experience. If you run a business, it will generally require at the minimum a little maintenance and leadership over the course of your time away, and that will keep you tied to your other life.

The time commitments of these activities may not be huge, but the psychological commitment will be. If you continue to check email and voice mail for six months, it's unlikely you'll be able to fully disconnect from your work, and fully connect with life around you. It also tends to diminish the perspective you achieve by leaving your work completely, and then returning to it. The emotions you feel when you first return to your job or business are a powerful insight into your true feelings.

If you're an *escaper*—you're trying to get away from work and other aspects of your life—then any obligations to your "normal" life will be draining for you. Conversely, though, if you're leaving work to pursue a freelance career, or some other type of activity, the same obligations may be energizing.

There's no right answer here. The trick is to listen to your heart. Don't keep part of your job and telecommute for six months because you're scared. Remember that your escape is about doing something new that you're passionate about.

Financial Escape Step #4: Cut Your Home Expenses

Just as important as the savings and income side of your sabbatical finances are the expenses on the opposite side of the ledger. Your hard-won savings can be quickly sucked dry if the costs of your regular life continue during your time off.

Fortunately you're taking a sabbatical, and that generally means you can cut your costs dramatically. If you plan to travel, you won't need your house or apartment, car, most of your wardrobe, and a host of related services like dry cleaning, cable TV, a maid, and your gym membership.

Note that this section is not about cutting your expenses *before* you escape. That's taken care of by setting up the automatic withdrawals from your account previously. You'll adjust your spending by default to accommodate them, saving you the distasteful process of budgeting and hoping to have a little extra to put aside each month (which rarely works).

So what's the goal? Your objective is to reduce the cost of your "normal" life to zero *during* your escape. That'll be essentially accomplished by taking care of two things:

1. *Reducing back-home sabbatical costs to zero for everything possible.* The big ones here are dealing with your home, your vehicles and your consumer debt.

2. *Pre-paying what you can't get down to zero.* This might include payments into retirement plans, insurance payments on vehicles in storage, fees to keep email accounts active, etc.

It's not rocket science to go through your expenses one by one and decide what you can cut while you're away—this isn't Budgeting 101. However, it's worth taking a look at some of the big ticket items. These are the ones that a) make a big difference financially and b) are often difficult to make decisions about because they tend to tie in to strong emotions.

Your Home

The largest asset for most people, your home is also highly emotionally charged. It represents financial security, progress, and a psychological grounding point. If they own their own home, many people can at least realize some measure of security in their later years regardless of other financial issues.

The issue here is not selling your home to fund your sabbatical. It's about dealing with the potential financial drain of real estate while you're away. As your largest asset, a home can also be your biggest liability, too. Here are some options for keeping your home, and keeping its costs down.

Rent Your Home

Your preferred option. You get to keep your investment intact, someone else makes the mortgage payments, and if all goes well, you'll get your utilities covered and make a little extra, too. You'll also get the added security of having someone living in your home, instead of it sitting empty, and you may be able to rent your home furnished, which saves you storing all your stuff.

If you're fortunate enough to own your home outright, then the finances of escaping become considerably easier; depending on how you take your sabbatical, you may be able to stay away indefinitely based only on rental income.

You can rent your home yourself, or most real estate agents will do it for you for a percentage of the take. They'll also take care of agreements and rent payments, too.

If you've never rented your home before, the first time is a bit strange. However, it's well worth it. The best advice is this: take the time to find the right tenant. Don't jump at the first person who comes along, just because they're interested. Do reference and credit checks, and consider carefully. In most cases, *no* tenant is better than a bad one.

Loan Your Home

If you can afford it, loaning your home to someone is an excellent solution. If you put the word out to your network, it's usually not that difficult to find a house-sitter. Having someone you trust in your home is very reassuring. They can watch the house, pay the bills, take care of repairs, and generally keep the place ship-shape while you're away. We've also used this option, and found that our home was in better shape when we returned.

Sell Your Home

Your home is likely the single largest expense you have each month. By the time you add up mortgage, taxes, insurance, utilities and maintenance, you're usually looking at a good chunk of your income.

Selling your home to eliminate those expenses is a viable option. Before you pound a real estate sign into the front lawn, though, here are a few questions to answer first:

- How long are you going for? Six months or less makes it pretty expensive to sell your home—agent and legal costs add up. Even a year is a short time period.

- Can you rent, lend or trade instead? That way, you can keep your asset intact.
- How's the market? Avoid selling in a down market. If the market's hot, however, perhaps you can get rid of your house, and make a tidy profit to fund your time away.
- Why aren't you renting your home? Is there no market for it, or is it an emotional reason?

Think carefully before you sell your home and use the equity to fund your escape. It needs to be the right choice for the right reason.

Trade/Swap Your Home

You'd be surprised how many people are trying to get *to* exactly where you're trying to escape *from*. The prospect of a home swap is not as far-fetched as it might seem, and with the internet, it's a whole lot easier than it ever was before.

The downside to swapping is that you're not really cutting the expense of a home out of your budget—you're essentially just swapping expenses, depending on the arrangement. However, if your sabbatical plans involve moving to an urban center, particularly an expensive one, then you may have to pay for accommodations anyway, and a home swap is worth considering.

There are internet resources galore for prospective home swappers, but one of the largest is www.homeexchange.com.

Cars and Other "Assets"

Although most people would consider their vehicles an asset, they're usually not. They cost money every month, and generally depreciate. Cars don't put money in your pocket, they take it out.

For this reason, it's often worthwhile selling vehicles and other cash-draining assets while you're away, particularly if your hiatus calls for anything longer than six months.

Debt

Consumer debt is a sabbatical-killer. If you've got a credit-card debt problem, you'll need to get on a program to solve it right now. Start a payment plan that'll get you done before you leave, and *get rid of the cards*. End of story.

Costs You Can't Escape

For ongoing costs like insurance, retirement plans and the like, use the following formula:

1. Take the total monthly amount of the bill in question
2. Multiply that by the number of months you'll be away
3. Divide the total by the number of months *until you leave*

For example, let's say you've got a $60 a month commitment to a life insurance policy that you'd like to maintain during your time away:

1. life insurance, $60/month
2. # of months of sabbatical: 6
3. # of months until you leave: 36

$60 x 6 months = $360
$360/36 months= $10

In this case, ten dollars is what you need to set aside each month between *now* and your departure date in order to cover the cost of the life insurance policy while you're gone.

You have two options for the monthly ten bucks: pay it into a savings account using the same auto-withdrawal system, or prepay the company in question, thereby slowly building a credit balance, which you can eat up while you're away. (Building a credit balance may seem silly to you, but for many people it's a safer solution than cash on hand in a savings account.)

Do this with as many ongoing expenses as you can manage. The objective is to avoid a savings hemorrhage right before you leave for your break. There are all kinds of last minute things you can find yourself cutting checks for, and the more of them you can predict, the better.

A Final Word on Cutting Home Expenses

As much as this section is about reducing the financial obligations of your regular life, there's also a larger picture here. Large assets are anchors to daily life, and as such, they become subconscious restrictions to *Belief*.

Without realizing it, we inhibit our idea of what is possible by virtue of where we are *now*. We immediately conceptualize our costs of taking a year off based on the costs of a year in our regular working life.

The two are not the same. Sabbatical math is different. The regular rules of finance don't apply. We were completely financially independent on our last sabbatical—meaning we could have stayed on sabbatical *forever*. Our tiny passive income was enough to cover our even tinier expenses. Back home, our passive income didn't cover the gas for our cars.

Cutting your home expenses while you're away can turn your sabbatical from a financial struggle into months of blissful financial independence.

Financial Escape Step #5: Find The Right Opportunity

There are an infinite number of ways to spend your time away. What you can do, see, enjoy, and experience is limited only by your imagination.

There's a close interplay, though, between how you decide to spend your sabbatical, and how much that escape will cost. For this reason, finding the right opportunity falls squarely in the money category.

If you've worked your way through the four secrets—Desire, Belief, Vision and Commitment—then you already know *what* you want to do. You just need to figure out the *how*. And no doubt, money is leading the list of questions on the tip of your tongue.

There's more than one way to skin a cat, as they say, and the expression applies as well to finances as it does felines. You want to do volunteer work with orphans? Excellent. You can do that on a budget of $0 a week or $2000 a week. This is no exaggeration—volunteering is a changing industry. Just the fact that it *is* an industry tells us something: there are lots of people willing to profit from your desire to get away.

There's nothing wrong with this. The fact that people are willing to profit from our desire to *eat* keeps grocery stores open—and there's nothing wrong with that. What you need to be aware of is that you don't *have* to pay $2000 a week to work with orphans.

The "new volunteerism", as I call it, is a rapidly growing industry of made-to-order, easy-to-enjoy work/travel opportunities for people with money, who want a volunteer experience. It's thriving on the growing demographic base of baby boomers with cash who want the satisfaction of feeding the hungry, saving the rainforest, and working in various second/third world scenarios. It's an easy way to travel and do good. It's also expensive.

If your time off includes travel and volunteering, these types of arrangements are very appealing—there's little risk, anxiety, or logistical work involved. It's so easy to simply provide your credit card and then enjoy the ride. And there's nothing wrong with it. But if your funds are limited, your year off can be slashed down to a month in no time. Fortunately, there are other options.

If you've followed the first steps of the financial process in this book, then by the time you escape you'll have found a way to reduce the cost of your life back home to as little as possible (preferably zero) while you're away, and you'll have an escape fund. This is where opportunity becomes important. Find an expensive opportunity, and you'll eat up your budget quickly, shortening your time, and adding to the stress of being away. Find an inexpensive opportunity, and you can practically escape forever.

Sabbatical math is different. It's difficult to grasp this completely while you're still immersed in your expensive, normal existence, but your life doesn't have to cost as much while you're on leave. Once you reduce your home life costs to zero, you can lead a profoundly simple, affordable and pleasurable life for the duration of your escape.

Note that this is not the same as living in poverty. Finding the right opportunity is about tapping into a type of economics that you may not be familiar with. Instead of what you're used to doing (trading your time at work in exchange for cash), you now have the freedom to explore all kinds of new options. You can exchange your time and expertise for accommodations, services, food, or whatever else you need. And strangely enough, it's not unusual to get more value for your time this way than you do at home.

The choice of how to spend your time away is yours. Just be aware that you don't have to spend a lot of cash if you don't want to. Part of escaping is breaking the link between time and money, and forging new bonds between time and things like health, relationships, and joy.

Your Sabbatical Opportunity

The best sabbaticals come in two forms. The first is a plan-free adventure. No agendas, bookings, or concrete plan. This kind of time away is about discovery and exploration—internal and external—and can be incredibly rewarding. It requires little more than a starting point.

The second form centers around a particular purpose, place or people. It's time off with a specific objective—volunteer work, language study, or a particular travel agenda, for example.

There are an infinite number of variations and combinations of both, and any given sabbatical can be made up of both planned and unplanned parts. For the moment, let's just say that each part of your time away can be distinguished by its level of organization or advance planning.

One is not better than the other, and the objective here is not to tell you how to plan. What's important to realize is that unless you plan to "wing it" for your entire time off, you'll need somewhere to go, and something to do. Finding that something, and ensuring that it's cost-effective, is called *finding your sabbatical opportunity*.

This is important for two reasons. First, the most legitimate, rewarding, and valuable opportunities aren't usually listed in the newspaper or on the internet. Yes, you can find plenty of them in those places, but they aren't necessarily the *best* ones. Second, finding a cost-effective way to do what you want to do with your sabbatical requires more than just booking a hotel.

Doing the "easy" thing when it comes to choosing how to spend your time away can be a fast ticket to poverty. It's easy to burn through all your savings in a couple of weeks by simply taking the first opportunity that comes along, or by not taking the time to find more options.

Consider for a moment your vision for your time away. Imagine it clearly.

Now know this: Right now, an incredibly cost-effective way to realize that opportunity is out there. You just have to reel it in.

How to Find Your Opportunity

You hear about them all the time—people who house-sit in the Caribbean, deliver yachts to the Mediterranean, train dolphins, work in orphanages, teach English in exotic places and more. Each of those people found an *opportunity*, and took it.

Most of them will be more than willing to share their stories—what it was like, how much it cost, who they met. What they might not tell you is *how* they found the opportunity in the first place. Not the "I met this guy" story, but the real process of how they came to meet the right person, or be in the right place at the right time.

It's not that they don't want to share the process with you, it's just that they may not realize there *is* one. They may chalk it up to luck, or that "things just worked out." The truth is that for most people who get what they want, there is a process at work; they don't realize they're using it. For them—the "naturals"—it's a subconscious process of *creating* luck.

What follows is a process that you can follow *consciously* and find the opportunity you need to make your sabbatical as pleasurable as you imagined, and as affordable as you hoped.

1. Get Clear about What You Want

After the Desire and Vision chapters of Part 1, you should have a pretty clear idea of what you're looking to do with your escape. Now's the time, however, to ensure that it's clear and concise.

There are literally hundreds of thousands of opportunities out there in the world—perhaps millions. In fact, if you believe in *creating* opportunities, then there's no end to the possibilities. The challenge is that the majority of them are floating around unknown, and unnamed. Getting clear in your mind about what you want provides an organizing principle. It helps you, and more importantly other people, sort out the appropriate from the inappropriate.

Boil your sabbatical down to one sentence that you can easily tell anyone. Your description should contain *where* you want to go, *how long* you want to go for, and *what* you plan to do. Here are some examples:

- "I'm going to spend two years teaching English in Japan."
- "We're going to do medical mission work in Africa for six months."
- "I'll be taking a year off to work in a vineyard in France."
- "I'm moving to Montana for six months to write a book."

You're going to start to put this sentence to work shortly. First, though, there are two important things to note. First of all, note the level of detail—not so specific as to limit you, but descriptive enough to create the picture. The *what's*, *where's* and *how long's* provide critical information to other people, and as you'll see shortly, those other people are critical in finding your sabbatical opportunity.

Second, each phrase is written as if it's pre-ordained. "I will do this," or "We're going to do that." There's no wishing, hoping, or wanting, just planned action. *This isn't pop psychology*—people are remarkably sensitive to language cues, and this is your way of telling them that you're not pipe-dreaming. You're serious, and serious intentions attract serious help. Don't be vague or tentative.

2. Identify the Deal Breakers

On the opposite side of the equation are the deal breakers. These are things you absolutely must, or must not have. If you *have* to go somewhere kid-friendly, then write that down. If it must be Spanish speaking, write that down.

Your deal breakers should be few and important. Their purpose is to help you assess opportunities as they arise. Try to remain as flexible as possible, but if there's something that's an absolute must or must not, write it down. This doesn't need to be in sentence format—it's not like your "elevator speech" in the previous step.

For our last sabbatical, we needed to have semi-regular internet access in order to stay in touch with business data. The businesses were self-sufficient, but we knew that we'd need to have internet access to keep an eye on the numbers and keep things growing. For us, that was one of just three clear deal breakers.

3. Know Your Strengths

In pursuing opportunities, it's helpful to know your strengths. While you may not need a resume for your sabbatical opportunity, any one of your various skills and traits could open a door for you. If you haven't done it in a while, you might consider making a resume even if you don't need one—it's a great way to open your mind to the broad range of strengths that you possess.

If it helps, break your strengths down into categories of hard skills, soft skills, and personal traits.

Hard skills are things like carpentry, computer programming, plumbing and open heart surgery. They include official qualifications like degrees and certificates, and unofficial qualifications—skills that you know you possess, period. It's important to note that these can be work and non-work related. If you're an exceptional tennis player, but you work as a computer programmer, then *both* of these are important skills.

Soft skills are less tangible abilities, like communication, conflict resolution, decision-making, management and leadership. They're often more general and abstract, but critically important.

Personal traits are the aspects of your disposition that make you...you. Are you agreeable? Adaptable? Confrontational? Shy? Outgoing? Friendly? Quiet? Loud?

Write them down. As with the other steps here, you don't have to *show* what you write to anyone—you're simply increasing your self-knowledge. Why? As doors start to open for you, you'll find that people become increasingly curious about you, your interests, your skills and your experiences. The better equipped you are to answer those questions, the wider the doors will open.

4. Talk it Up

Of all the steps, this is the most crucial. It's really *networking*, but don't get caught up in any negative associations you might have with the word—this is actually much, much easier, and a lot more fun.

Let's start by clarifying one thing: the most important part of finding the right sabbatical opportunity is *other people*. If finding the courage and drive to take a year off is a personal journey, then finding the most cost-effective way to spend that time off is an *interpersonal* one; it requires other people, and the more the better.

This part of finding your opportunity is fun and easy:

a. *Tell Everyone.* Start spreading the word, sharing your news, bragging, or whatever helps you get the word out to as many people as possible.

b. *Be Specific.* Use your one-sentence pitch, and fill in the rest as time allows.

c. *Ask for Missing Pieces.* If you need to find a contact in an industry, country, etc., make sure you mention that to people.

d. *Follow the Leads.* You won't have to talk to many people before someone says, "Oh! My cousin is working in Ecuador right now. You should talk to her." In these cases—and you'll be surprised how often it happens—make sure you follow up right away.

Here's a critical thing to remember: people love to hear about this kind of thing, and they love to help even more. You won't be imposing, and you won't have to drag the information out of them. In most cases all they're doing is referring you to someone else, and feeling great about doing it.

5. Stay Big Picture

As opportunities begin to crop up, it'll be tempting to focus on the details right away. Don't. Stay at 40,000 feet. If your friend refers you to a cousin, your first question doesn't have to be "Are the beds twins or doubles?"

It's not that you can't get to the details eventually, or that they're not important. The issue is that depending on what you're doing, the details may not *exist*. Part of the sabbatical mind shift is learning to move from detail to big picture. From close-up, to panorama.

Focusing on tiny details also tends to make you of less interest to people who might be able to provide you with opportunities. For comparison, imagine your task right now is to hire an assistant to help you with your current job, or in your home. You place an ad in the paper, and receive two phone calls. The first person asks about your job, and how they might help, and briefly mentions their qualifications. The second caller starts the conversation with a single question. "What's the salary?"

Which caller do you think you'll be most interested in talking to?

Learn to trust. Trust your instinct to know which opportunity is best for you, and trust that whatever happens, you'll be able to handle it, *sans* details.

An Example

Our last sabbatical opportunity (the one that cost $150 a *month* for food and accommodation) was found by following these five exact steps.

Get Clear

We dedicated a great deal of time to just dreaming about our sabbatical, and had arrived at a very clear idea of what we wanted:

- Something tropical to semi-tropical
- A Spanish speaking country
- Nearby children for our daughter to play with

Our one sentence description looked like this:

We're taking six months off in a tropical country where our daughter can make local friends and we can all learn to speak Spanish together.

In our case, we weren't particular about the exact location, just the climate and language.

Deal Breakers

There were three deal breakers for us. The first was that there had to be other kids—no kids, no deal. The second was that the country had to be relatively safe and welcoming to outsiders. We weren't interested (for this trip) in closed societies or civil wars. Finally, as mentioned, we needed periodic internet access.

Strengths

We had a pretty clear idea of ours going in. We'd spent time discussing what we had to offer to various opportunities, and what we'd like to do with our time. We placed particular emphasis on our desire to "be of use", our flexibility, and the breadth of our skill base.

Talk It Up

We'd planned our most recent escape about five years in advance, and had been telling people about it the whole time—not in an active "networking" sense, but in the way you'd tell any good friend or family member about your future plans. Just about everyone knew someone in another country, and it was easy to find contacts.

Big Picture

Here's exactly what happened. A friend was collecting shoes for charity, and I stopped by her office to drop off a pair. I mentioned our trip, and asked where the shoes were going. She referred me to a brochure on the wall for a charity in South America, with a local contact.

I went home and emailed the address on the brochure. I got a reply the next day from the guy running the shoe collection project, and we met for coffee. I told him about us, our skills and interests, and he told me about his mission work. We met twice more for coffee, and that was it—the next time I saw him was when he picked us up at the airport in Paraguay. No contracts, no nitty-gritty details.

It was a remarkable, rewarding, and incredibly inexpensive sabbatical. And it was all arranged on coffee and a handshake within a few minutes of our rural home.

How critical is finding the right opportunity? For that matter, how critical is finding *any* specific opportunity? The answer is that it depends on your budget and your objective. If you've got cash reserves and just want to wander around and see what happens, then no one needs to provide you with an opportunity—you can provide your own, and have a fantastic time.

However, if cash is tight and you've got some specific requirements, then the opportunity becomes critical to success. Remember that the world is on your side in this game. People love to help, and the number of opportunities greatly outnumber the number of people like you who have the desire and commitment to fill them.

When Money's Not the Problem

It may surprise you to learn that for many people, lack of money is not the single biggest obstacle to getting away. In fact, for many people, it's not even on the radar.

The level of wealth in developed nations has exploded over the last decade. The number of millionaires is skyrocketing. Sure, the money may not be evenly distributed, but there's no denying that there's a whole lot of it out there.

What's surprising, though, is not that so much wealth exists, but that the people who have it have just as tough a time getting away as those who don't.

Wealth can be a serious barrier to escape. The thought of losing everything can seem a lot more daunting when everything is *a lot*. Those with few resources have less to lose, financially, and a shorter path to getting it back again.

If you have the money and the desire to leave, but can't seem to do so, then spend some extra time on the first section of the book; your escape also begins on the inside, and the four secrets will help you find a path to your dream escape. At any price.

ESCAPING YOUR JOB

Your work is to discover your world and then with all your heart give your-self to it.

-Buddha

A Japanese policeman, distraught by working long hours and weekends for two months, stabbed himself in the stomach with a knife to get some time off, police said Monday.

Associated Press, June 6, 2007

I N THE 1999 COMEDY *Office Space*, Ron Livingstone plays Peter Gibbons, the incredibly miserable software engineer who can't seem to catch a break. After a visit to a hypnotist renders him completely free of all worry in the workplace, Peter takes a radical step in his approach to work: he simply stops showing up. As downsizing consultants cull the workforce, Peter spends his days in stress-free bliss chasing true love.

Peter's ultimate attitude toward work is revealed in his interview with Bob Porter, one of the consultants hired to decide who will be laid off in the company's downsizing:

Bob: "It looks like you've been missing a lot of work lately."

Peter: "I wouldn't say I've been missing it, Bob."

It's a hilarious, poignant moment, and ironically, Peter's attitude actually nets him some big points with the consultants. And while "not showing up" one day isn't the ideal strategy for dealing with a sabbatical from work, there's a lesson to be learned from *Office Space*: life is short, and work is long. Take a break from it all. Enjoy some carefree days, and you might just find you come out ahead in the long run. Like the tortoise and the hare, it's not always the fastest (or most stressed or miserable) who wins the race.

Although sabbatical tales are not hard to find, it's somewhat more challenging to find anyone whose story is one of regret. Most people claim no career damage; what's more, many people insist that their sabbatical gave them a boost, either in their existing job, or in a new and improved career.

I can *tell* you that, but the reality is that after money, the issue of how to deal with work is generally the next biggest sabbatical rock to move. If you're on a career track, or you've been at the same job for a long period of time, the thought of leaving can be pretty scary. If you don't *like* your job, then quitting might be enticing, but still scary, nonetheless.

And for those who absolutely love their work, the situation can be even tougher. How are you going to give up your daily passion for any length of time? For the work-lovers and workaholics, the challenge is different but equally daunting.

The good news, however, is that unlike the Japanese policeman, you don't need to stab yourself to get a break; there are effective alternatives.

This chapter is designed to help navigate the thorny issue of leaving work *temporarily*—it's for the people who intend to return to their job, or at least keep relationships intact until they return to the workforce. If you can't stand your job, and are desperately *wanting* to quit, then you may not need most of what follows. You might mind, however, that what follows is valuable for keeping relationships intact, and finding win-win solutions for everyone.

As with money issues, the first step in dealing with your work is to open your mind to a variety of outcomes. Simply quitting and walking away is only one solution of many; don't assume you'll have to choose it. You might, for example, come back to the same job. You might return to a different position with the same company. You might get paid while you're away. You might work part-time, or complete a special project while on sabbatical. There are innumerable ways to maintain and nurture your current work situation while you're gone. What's important is that you start the process sooner as opposed to later. Springing your sabbatical plans on your boss at the last minute is not going to help the situation. Advance planning and ongoing dialogue are the best way to reach an outcome that will send you off with a clear conscience and a stress-free mind.

Note: *If you're a business owner, you're likely getting ready to skip to the next chapter. You might consider giving this a skim first—there are some aspects that might apply to your business if you have partners or other invested parties.*

Negotiating Your Escape Part 1: 4 Big Questions before You Start

If you'd like to return to your current job after your leave, then you're about to enter what is essentially a *negotiation*. Don't let the word scare you—a negotiation for our purposes is nothing more than two (or more) parties trying to agree on something. Negotiation is likely something you've done all your life, but didn't realize it.

(Even if you're *not* planning to return to your current job, there may still be things to negotiate before you go (severance, vacation pay, etc.) and it's *always* in your best interest to not burn any bridges. In other words, don't skip this part because you hate your job.)

Before you break the good news to your colleagues and start cutting deals with your boss, we need to take a close look at your thoughts and attitudes about the whole leave-your-job scenario. Before you even *think* about opening discussions at work, make sure you're very clear on your answers to the following questions.

Question 1: Are you negotiating terms, or asking permission?

This is a critical question. Are you asking *permission* to go on sabbatical, or are you trying to negotiate the best possible terms for what you feel is a "done deal"? These are very different mindsets, and your answer indicates the level of commitment to your sabbatical, and how well you'll do in the negotiation.

If you're asking your employer if you *can* take an extended leave, you're likely to get a quick "no". If you're *telling* your employer you are, and would like to discuss how to make that work in your company's favor, then you're as good as on your way.

(Don't let the term *telling* throw you off. We're looking at your internal attitudes right now, not your actual words. Naturally, you're not going to barge in and pull a "take this job and shove it" routine, but for best results you need to be in the headspace of *I'm going*, as opposed to *I hope they let me go*.)

And what if you *are* asking permission? That's okay, just be aware that you'll need to be more persistent and start sooner, and that your position is not as strong as it would be if you view (internally, at least) your departure as a fact.

Question 2: Are you willing to walk?

In any form of negotiation, there's one secret that will give you an edge every time: *be willing to walk*. There is nothing so empowering and emotionally freeing as having the confidence to simply walk away from your job. Being detached from the outcome puts you in an incredibly strong position, and it shows in your demeanor. *Ironically, being willing to walk frequently means you don't have to.*

Is this necessary? Do you need to be willing to walk in order to get what you want? No. But being willing puts you in a very strong position. This may not be easy for you, but consider this: if you *must* be able to return to your job after your sabbatical, then your employer essentially has unlimited power to control all the terms of the deal. If returning to the same job is the only option you're willing to consider, then your boss gets to dictate all the terms. You'll have little choice but to go along with what they offer.

You may be able to put on a good poker face, but in the end you'll ask for less and get less than if you're willing to walk away from it all.

Realistically, this isn't for everyone. You may have years invested in a career and a company, and be, understandably, unwilling to walk away from that. That's okay. Your sabbatical is still yours to take.

Can you *become* willing to walk? The answer is yes. The only difference between the *you* that's not willing to leave your job, and the *you*
that is willing, is mindset. Being willing to walk away is, put most
simply, a matter of changing your mind.

Step outside yourself for a moment. Imagine that you're being
forced to debate with *yourself* the merits of abandoning your current
career. Your job is to build a convincing argument for not returning to
work.

To build that argument, start generating a list of every positive
thing that would or could happen if you didn't have to return to the
same job after your sabbatical. If it helps, divide the list into two parts:
bad things that will stop, and good things that could start.

Bad Things That Will Stop

- Boredom
- Office politics
- Difficult co-workers, managers, staff, etc.
- Commutes
- Traffic
- Uncomfortable office conditions
- Unethical work
- Low pay
- Poor benefits
- Long/inconvenient hours
- Clients, projects and tasks you don't like
- Fear of being fired, downsized, etc.

Good Things That Can Start

- Better pay
- Passionate work
- More time with family
- Time to be more healthy
- More time for hobbies, friends, and other outside interests
- Great colleagues
- Safer, easier, or more ethical work
- A new business venture

As you build your list, start arguing this position: *Leaving that job would be the best thing that could ever happen because:*

Start imagining what could happen in a *new* job or role that had all the pros and none of the cons of your current one.

And decide: *are you willing to walk away?*

If the answer is no, that's fine. Just make sure you know the answer, and understand its implications.

Question 3: What's Not Negotiable?

Although pop psychology might tell you to go with your first answer, there's a potential pitfall here. You've dedicated much time to envisioning your sabbatical in all its glorious, palm-studded detail, but how much thought have you given to what happens *after?* The way in which you leave your work will have a great impact on what happens when you return.

So, before you ask yourself this question, let's rephrase it in a different way: what do you *really* want? What do you really, really, really want? Are you sure you want to quit your job forever? Are you sure you want to come back to your job?

Take the time to decide precisely what you want your work to be like when you return. Some of the details might include:

- Duration
- Salary
- Benefits
- Position you'll return to
- Obligations during your time away

Now ask yourself, "What are the deal breakers?" If you *must* have your original job back when you return, then so be it. Just remember that you'll have to make that clear, and that each deal breaker you have makes it a little harder to get away. *Flexibility increases your likelihood of escape.*

Question 4: Why Should They Negotiate?

People will not negotiate with you unless they believe you can help them or hurt them. If your leaving has zero perceived effect on a company, then there's not much reason to start a dialogue. Most employers, though, are inclined to see your departure as somewhere between mildly negative, and crushing. If your hiatus is a real blow to your organization, than they'll be anxious to discuss your *staying*. Staying, however, is not what you're after. You're *leaving*. If your boss is solely focused on how to negotiate against that, you're going to be working at odds with each other.

In most cases, your boss is going to need your help seeing the positive side of things. To ensure that your employer is a) willing to negotiate, and b) willing to discuss the terms of you *leaving*, as opposed to *staying*, you'll have to demonstrate your commitment to leaving, and then pitch in some brainpower on the positive side.

Here are just a few advantages that your time away may hold for your boss/company—you'll likely be able to get far more specific for your particular scenario.

Bring Back Added Value. You could use your sabbatical to improve your skills, learn new technologies, or study a possible new market.

Extend Your Lifespan. A sabbatical could keep you from quitting, burning out, or switching firms. Better to lose you for a few months then to lose you forever.

Save Money. You might save the company money by leaving during a slow season in the industry, for example.

Help Recruit. If your company is growing, you can find and train your replacement. This makes your departure less painful, and helps grow the company workforce in the long run.

For all these negotiation questions, you'll be better equipped if you do your homework. Does your company have a sabbatical policy? Are there precedents for other people having done this? Are there remote working/telecommuting options or precedents? Where's your industry headed? What skills are fading? Which ones are in demand? What's the employment market like? What are the details of your benefit/retirement plans?

The more you know going into negotiations, the better equipped you'll be to respond to objections, and generate positive alternatives.

Negotiating Your Escape Part 2: Guiding Principles

While the four questions are about getting very clear on you and your employer's goals and options before you start a dialogue, the following negotiation principles are guidelines for steering your conversation.

Primum non nocere: First, Do No Harm

One of the principal precepts taught to medical students is that of *primum non nocere*: first do no harm. It urges physicians to consider the possible harm of a treatment or course of action.

In considering how to approach your job or career, *primum non nocere* is worth keeping in mind. After all—going into negotiations with the idea of losing something is certainly not going to help your position. Don't burn any bridges. There's no need, and nothing to be gained. Regardless of the decisions made, there's no reason you can't maintain good relationships within your company and industry. Commit to doing no harm whenever possible.

Start Early

Three years to go until departure? Tell your boss now.

Starting early has several advantages, the first of which is that it's completely non-threatening. Telling your employer that you're leaving in three years doesn't start any fires—it's too far away to worry about. It's too soon to start negotiating, and most employers will think you're pipe-dreaming. Your revelation, though, has put the idea "out there" so that it's no longer a secret. As time passes, and you casually bat the idea around the office a few more times, it starts to slowly gel into a *fact*. "Wow—you just got back from Mexico? We're planning a six-month trip there in a few years. Any places you'd recommend?"

More importantly, starting discussions early dovetails nicely with our critical strategy of *talking it up*. Remember that spreading the word is a key component of commitment, and it's also crucial to finding the right opportunity, which is in turn a key piece of the financial puzzle (see how this all works?). Keeping your hiatus secret makes it harder to put the four secrets to work, and reduces your odds of finding a financially-feasible sabbatical opportunity.

You may be wondering, "What if they fire me or pass me over for promotion because they know I'm leaving?" It's possible, but being open and honest is more professional. That being said, every company is different. If you feel the need to wait until a strategic time to break the news to your employer, and you have a reason to think it's smart to do so, go for it. In my world, if you work at a company where you get fired for proposing a sabbatical three years down the road, it'll likely be the best thing that ever happened to you.

Think Win-Win

Resist the natural temptation to see this as an all or nothing scenario, with either you or your employer coming out on top. Think in terms of finding a solution that results in everyone walking away feeling good about the terms.

Set the Right Tone

Adversarial negotiations don't tend to deliver win-win outcomes. Keep the tone positive, friendly and respectful, but be firm in how important this is to you.

Start High

A basic tenet of negotiation is to start high. If you want six months off, ask for a year, and then you've got room to move.

Don't Make it Personal

This isn't about last year's rotten bonus, the pay raise you didn't get, or your boss's horrible management record. Well, okay, maybe it *is* in your case, but that's not going to help your negotiation. This is about making a change in your life. Even if it is *because* of your boss, don't make that part of the dialogue. Try to keep personal issues out of it.

Remember the Decision-Maker

Although, as mentioned, you want to find the benefit to the company to help your negotiating position, remember that in most cases, the decision to yay or nay your sabbatical lies with one person. You'll need to make a pitch to that decision maker. If your sabbatical can make your company money, or cut costs, that's fine, but if those outcomes don't help your immediate manager (or whoever the decision-maker is) than they won't have much of an impact.

Know Who the Asset Is

Remember that *you* are the one that they pay. You're the person who provides the service that the company pays for. If they didn't value that, they wouldn't be paying you. Don't be fooled into parent-child thinking. Employment is a business agreement between adults. Don't be intimidated.

Be Persistent

It's not uncommon to get a negative first response to your sabbatical plans from the powers-that-be. Don't let that stop you. Be persistent. Sabbatical stories are ripe with tales of finally "wearing down the boss" enough to get permission to go. Don't let a *no* dampen your enthusiasm or slow your progress.

Don't Wait: Keep the Sabbatical Machine Going

It's important that while you're negotiating, you keep momentum moving on your escape plan. Keep working on the financials. Keep looking for your opportunity. *Behave as if it's happening.* Not only will it keep you from losing valuable time "waiting for permission", but it'll help your mental game. Do *not* wait for a green light from work before starting the rest of your leave preparations.

CB

Make no mistake: leaving a career you've invested many years in is going to feel like a *very* big rock to get moving.

If it helps to break it down, you're really looking at three options. The first is to leave your job, and return to it after your hiatus. The second is to leave your job permanently. Since you can always change your mind and choose the second one anytime you please, it usually makes sense best to pursue the first option.

The trick is *not* to choose the third option, which is to never leave.

Be brave. Start the dialogue. Remember that *there's nothing wrong with what you're considering*. And if you really do need a break from work, then it's best for you *and* your company that you take it. In the long run, everyone wins.

You can learn a lot about your employer from her attitude towards your proposal. If, for example, she'd rather lose you than let you take a leave of absence without pay, what does that say about how a company values your contribution? How secure is that paycheck if your company is has no qualms about replacing you permanently based on your desire to better yourself?

Trust your instincts. If your escape is calling, then pay attention. There's a reason.

For further advice on negotiating time away, consider reading *Six Months Off*, listed in the recommended reading section at the back of this book.

LEAVING YOUR BUSINESS

One of the symptoms of an approaching nervous breakdown is the belief that one's work is terribly important.

-Bertrand Russell

I think that maybe inside any business, there is someone slowly going crazy.

-Joseph Heller
Something Happened

RUNNING A BUSINESS PRESENTS an enormous challenge for many people who'd like to take time away; it's a *really* big rock. If you've invested your savings and built a business from scratch, or if you feel that keeping your business afloat takes every waking minute you have, the thought of taking a sabbatical probably only flickers in your mind briefly on the second day of a rare long weekend holiday.

You're not alone. While much of the working world dreams of owning their own business, those who *do* know how physically and mentally draining it can be. There are many, many business owners like you who would all use the same word to describe taking six months or more off from their business: *impossible*. Who'd run the place? Who'd bring in the sales? Who'd take care of the *money*? It's impossible!

Wrong.

If you've got the smarts, guts and gumption to build your business to the extent you have, you can take a sabbatical. (Heck, you probably *deserve* one by now.)

Not only that, but *taking extended time off might just be the best thing that ever happened to you and your business.*

Think *that's* impossible? Welcome to *Escape 101*, where all things are possible. You're about to discover why not showing up at the office is going to make you happier, healthier, *and* wealthier. Interested? Follow me—but no briefcases allowed...

The Greatest Business Secret of All Time

Confession time: there's some selling going on here. You're a business owner, though, so selling you on the emotional benefits of a longer vacation is likely not going to work. Your spouse has probably already tried.

However, selling you on the *business* benefits might just do the trick.

To discover the business benefits of getting out of Dodge, let's start here: *do you actually have a business?*

This may sound like a crazy question, but a true "business" is distinctly different from other similar entities. You might be self-employed, or do freelance work on your own schedule, and call it a business, but is it really? In *Rich Dad's Cashflow Quadrant*, Robert Kiyosaki discusses what makes a true "business":

> *"Those who are true "B's" (Business Owners) can leave their businesses for a year or more, and return to find their business more profitable and running better than when they left. In a true self-employed type business, if the "S" (Self-Employed) left for a year or more, the chances are there would be no business left to return to."*

> *"So what causes the difference? Saying it simply, an "S" (Self-Employed) owns a job. A "B" (Business Owner) owns a system and then hires competent people to operate the system. Or, put another way, in many cases the S (Self-Employed) is the system. That is why they cannot leave."*[14]

To put it more simply, if your business makes money while you're on vacation, it's a business. If you need to be *in* your business all the time for it to operate, then *you're not running a business. You own a job.*

That's okay—many people do quite well owning a job. Common "job owners" include:

- Doctors
- Lawyers
- Accountants, bookkeepers
- Consultants
- Freelance writers, designers and artists
- Small contractors and construction companies
- Small family businesses
- Most businesses with no employees
- Individuals who sell their time/charge by the hour/day/week

There are many people in that list making a small fortune every year. Job owners all have one thing in common, though: *they don't get paid when they're not working.*

What does this mean to your sabbatical? It means one critical thing: if you *own a job*, then it will provide you with zero income while you're away. Without you there, the business generates no money. If you own a business, however, you can earn while you're gone, and come back to a thriving operation.

What if you don't own a business by this definition? Then you've got three choices for escaping:

1. *Walk away.* Shut your doors and accept the corresponding hit in income.
2. *Sell the business.*
3. *Transition into a true business.*

All the options are perfectly viable. Walking away may be just what the doctor ordered, and I'm not going to advise against it. Selling is a great option, too, but if you don't already have a true business, you'll need to find someone else who wants to own a job.

The third option, transitioning to a true business, not only allows you to *keep* your business, but it offers some other less obvious perks. Here are the top three *permanent* (they last after your sabbatical is over) benefits of developing your true business:

Business Benefit #1: Income

More specifically, this benefit is "income from your business when you're not there". True business owners are able to earn income from their business without being on the job, in the office, or even in the country. And they're able to do it with a minimal time investment in overseeing what's happening. In exchange, they receive profits, a salary and/or other benefits.

If you haven't yet experienced the joy of building something that earns income for you when you're not working, get ready to be happy.

Business Benefit #2: Growth

The real economic difference between owning a business and owning a job is the effect of *multipliers*. When you hire other people to work in your business, and introduce systems and technology for them to do work more efficiently, you're increasing the amount of products and services that can be supplied in the same amount of time.

Most job-owners are limited by time. They have only 24 hours in a day in which to work. Adding more people multiplies the amount of work that can be done in that same 24 hours, whether it's selling a product, manufacturing it, or providing a service. By adding more people and infrastructure in the right amounts, you can continue to multiply.

When you transition to a true business, you instantly turn on a multiplying effect that can allow your business to grow in ways it never could have before.

Business Benefit #3: Sale Value

Transitioning to a true business allows you to build an asset that's worth something to sell. There's a vibrant market for selling businesses, but the value of those businesses drops off sharply if the business owner has to do all the work. If you can build a business that works in your absence, with a minimum of management on your part, you'll have an asset that you can quite easily sell if you ever choose to.

So what is the Greatest Business Secret of All Time? It's this: *removing "you" from day-to-day business operations is essential to long term business growth and health.* Read that carefully: it's *business* growth and health.

Obviously removing you from day-to-day management can create more *personal* growth and health, but that's not the secret. The trick is that removing you is good for the *business*.

It may be hard to see this from where you stand right now, but your sabbatical might be just the thing to take your business to the next level. And what's the best part of all the benefits above? *They continue after you return.* That means that in your post-escape life, you can balance your work and personal life the way you want to, not the way your business demands.

Objective: Transition to a True Business

> *Once you recognize that the purpose of your life is not to serve your business, but that the primary purpose of your business is to serve your life, you can then go to work on your business, rather than in it...*

> -Michael E. Gerber
> *The E-Myth Revisited*

So what do you do if you don't have a true business according to our definition? Or if you do have a true business, but can't imagine leaving it for such an extended period? If the benefits I've mentioned get you fired up, consider transitioning your current practice or operation into a true business.

This transition to true business can seem incredibly daunting. Many job-owners can't escape the "self-employment" level of business because of how they *think* about their businesses; they simply can't imagine the business running without them.

They're probably right. In its present form, their business likely *can't* operate without them at the helm. Your job is to change that for your business. Whether you've got a "true" business or not, your exit plan requires that your operation runs without you.

After all, you're not going to be there, are you?

Let's get started.

From Business to Sabbatical in Four Steps

The idea that your business can operate without you isn't as crazy as it sounds. It takes a little determination and elbow grease, but, as with most things, it really takes the right *thinking* more than anything. Remember, thousands of people before you have done this. How else do companies of all sizes, across all industries continue to make profits after their owners have retired, or moved on to other businesses?

The four steps below will get your brain in the right mode, and help you take the practical steps necessary to leave (and return to) a prosperous business.

Step 1: The Letter

As you're no doubt accustomed to by now, we'll be starting your business transition on the *inside.* That's where the real barriers are.

Suspend your disbelief, grant yourself a few free minutes to dream, and imagine the following scenario. (It works even better doing it with a partner, spouse, or other people whose input you respect. More heads are often better than one, and other people won't be as embroiled in the day-to-day operations that make it difficult to see possibilities for change.)

Here's the scenario. A letter arrives for you. To your surprise (and curiosity), you discover it comes from your long-estranged, and disgustingly wealthy Uncle Gustav. He's somehow caught wind of your sabbatical dreams. (How, you're not sure, but you suspect it's something to do with the last family reunion that you'd rather forget right now.)

Uncle Gustav's estranged and filthy rich for a reason: he worked his fingers to the bone for nearly 60 years and never spent a penny. While this may have made him rich, it has also made him friendless and miserable. Now, in his 80th year, he's ill, regretful, and repentant.

Uncle Gustav doesn't want you to make the same mistakes he has. In a letter written from his deathbed, he offers you a challenge.

Dear Niece,

Sixty years ago I started the business that would grow into Gustav, Inc. It has made me wealthy beyond my wildest dreams, but I realize now it hasn't made me happy.

I see myself in you. Hardworking. Passionate. Energetic. Self-reliant. Entrepreneurial is the word they use these days, I suppose. But in those traits, I also see the seeds of disaster that led me to where I am now: rich, but old, tired and unhappy.

What I know now is that it didn't have to be this way. I could have run my business without running myself into the ground. I could have taken more time for friends, family and other passions without losing my company. It's as clear to me now as it was murky then.

While my time is limited, my other resources are not. To get to the point, I'd like to offer you ten million dollars to leave your business for six months, and take this sabbatical of yours, whatever it might be. Take the time. Enjoy your family while they'll still allow it.

Life is short. I hope you consider my offer. I'm sure you won't regret it.

G.

P.S. Should I expire before you decide, the details are attached. My lawyers will answer any questions.

Wow! you think, *This is fantastic! Ten million dollars!* Then you stop. *But what about leaving the business?* Ah! *No problem*, you realize. With ten million coming down the pipe, you can walk away permanently. You're rich! As you walk into the living room to tell your husband the good news, you flip idly to the second page, and peruse the details.

And that's where you find the catch. It's right there in paragraph four:

My niece may not be physically present in the offices, and can only contact her business once per week. Less would be better, but I can live with that.

No problem, right? You're not planning on checking in at *all*! But then your eyes skim on to paragraph five:

Over the six months in question, the business must break even or be profitable.

Your husband enters the room, and sees your face. "What's the matter?" With a strange mix of excitement and fear, you tell him the news, and the two of you sit down and chat long into the night.

Putting The Letter to Work

Uncle's Gustav's letter is no joke. The biggest challenge facing business owners is the attitude that "it can't be done". The purpose of The Letter is to get you into a state of mind where you can freely consider the *possibility* that this could really work.

Allow yourself to consider the proposition seriously. If there *were* ten million dollars at stake, what could you do to free yourself from your business while still allowing it to flourish?

And note two critical aspects of Uncle Gustav's proposition. First, the business has to break even or better. Second, you *are* allowed to check in. Unlike an employee who has left work behind, your business is still an asset to be nurtured while you're away. The employee can walk away while someone else runs the show. You'll likely want to at least keep tabs on progress. To that end, let's redefine "leaving your business" in sabbatical terms:

Leaving your business for sabbatical means your business at least breaks even, and that you contact your team no more than once a week. Any more than that, and you're not really on sabbatical—you're telecommuting from wherever you are, and it just ain't the same.

The key shift in thinking you need to make here is to begin to think of yourself as a business *owner*, not a *manager*. Managers are, by necessity, heavily involved in day-to-day business activities. Owners are only involved to the extent they choose to be. Owners *hire* managers.

Don't let the simplicity of the scenario fool you. Play along. Let your mind explore the options. Don't disregard any idea immediately. Free your mind from "can't" and "impossible". Take as long as you need—an hour, a day, or a week. And when you've got an idea of how you might pull this off, and claim Uncle Gustav's prize, move on to the next step.

Step Two: Systems

If you gave Uncle Gustav's letter it's due, you've probably realized by now that you need to replace yourself in your business so that you're not doing the work of the business, and you're not there overseeing how *other* people do the work of your business.

To do that requires *people* and *systems*—they are the engine of your business. True businesses are really machines for creating money—it's as simple as that. In one end of the machine you pour resources—time, raw materials, labour, money, brains and ideas. Along the way you add sales and customers and service, and eventually, dollars flow out the other end.

Like all machines, yours requires specific parts and processes for doing the job of creating money. If you took the gear shift out of your car and replaced it with a banana—that machine (your car) would suddenly become far less effective at its job (getting you from A to B). The same applies to your business. If you don't know what to add where, things are going to go off the rails.

The specific parts and processes of your business, and how they interact, are called systems. If you haven't transitioned to a true business, then right now every system is probably in your head. All the information about how the machine works is locked up inside your brain. You *are* the machine.

The trick to getting away from your business, regardless of its size and effectiveness, is to ensure that systems are in place so that when you remove yourself from the machine, it continues to function. *You need to stop being the machine.*

For our escape plan, we're going to work with four different types of systems: *operational*, *growth*, *reporting*, and *contingency*. You can use any terms you like, but what we're trying to do is capture the essential broad functions of your business.

Operational Systems

Operational systems are things that run your business. How goods are manufactured. How services are provided. How bills are paid. How phones are answered. How materials and supplies are ordered.

Most businesses, particularly small ones, have no set process for how many of these things operate. They happen as needed, or when something critical happens that forces them to be addressed. In many small businesses, the owner is actually doing *all* of them. To escape, you'll need to define set rules for how everything in your business operates, so that it can be done the same way over and over, by someone else.

Operational systems are about removing *you* from two areas of the business: day-to-day *tasks*, and day-to-day *decision-making*.

Tasks

With the exception of the things we're going to specify later, everything you do in your day-to-day work life will need to be done by someone else. *Everything.*

How do you do this? First, you'll need to *capture* the tasks you work on. You can start by brainstorming a list of everything you do on a day-to-day basis. It's likely, however, that you won't be able to capture everything in one sitting, so you'll want to keep a notebook or computer file that you can add to regularly. Keep updating that file for a week or two, or until you feel like you've captured most of the tasks that you perform.

And now? Now someone else needs to do those tasks. To accomplish this, every item on that list needs the following information:

- An objective, or goal
- A new person to do it (the *owner)*
- How frequently it should be done
- Approximately how long it should take
- Instructions for how to do it

Keep the list handy. Your lists, and the ones to follow, will help you decide your *people* needs—who will do what, whether you need more people, and whether those people need to improve their skills. Your list is the skeleton of an operations manual for your business.

Decision-Making

A classic difference between entrepreneurs and employees is their affinity for decision-making. Many employees don't want to make hard decisions—they see it as *your* job. And while that may be currently true, you can't escape your business and still make all the decisions.

Downloading decision-making is all about empowering people. The people who run the show in your absence are going to need to be able to make these decisions on their own.

For every single question or decision that you make in the course of daily operations, ask yourself what you have to do to not have to make the same decision again.

There are two types of decisions you need to *stop* making: the ones you currently make for your own role, and the ones you currently make for other people in your business who can't or won't make those decisions themselves.

The second type is where you'll start. Develop the habit of not making decisions for other people. Simply respond to all requests for decisions with, "What do you think?" If the person can't decide, ask them to come back when they have a recommendation. If they need more information, ensure that they get it, but do not make the decision on their behalf.

Once your team begins to make their own decisions, you'll be in a position to start to offload some of those other decisions (the ones on your plate) to your new and improved, decision-capable staff.

Growth Systems

It's been said that a business can only be in one of two states: growth or decline. "Status quo" doesn't really exist in the open market, and the one area in which your business will be most at risk during your absence is in its ability to expand.

Small businesses are particularly dependant on their owners to drive sales, and while you'll discover that with a little dedication and delegation you can make yourself redundant in many areas of your business, growth needs some special attention on its own. Without it, you'll find your sabbatical freedom slowly eroding over the course of your absence as your business shrinks.

So how do you continue to gain new clients or customers, and ensure that existing ones remain as patrons? The first step is to develop a systematic process for growth, just like with operations.

First, capture all the growth-creating activities for your business.

For example, if advertising, sending a flyer, calling on sales accounts, or offering an annual sale have traditionally worked in the past, then you'll want to ensure those same things continue in your absence. If regular innovation and product development is critical to annual growth, then that needs to be part of the system.

Next, systemize those activities

For each of these critical growth activities, build a system just like you did for operations: define the *objectives*, *activities*, *timelines*, and *owner* for each, and review them with your staff.

The second step to ensuring continued expansion during your absence is to provide incentives for growth. Many business owners feel that no one cares about their business as much as they do. To some extent, this is true (it's your baby, after all), but nowhere is it more true than in the area of growth. While it's relatively easy to pay someone to complete operational tasks, it's more challenging to impress upon employees the importance of growth.

By adding bonuses, commissions, ownership and other performance related perks, you provide ways to move employee thinking from the operations side of your business to the growth side. If your staff isn't focused on growth, it's not going to happen in your absence.

Reporting Systems

Since you won't be in the office during your sabbatical, and will only be able to check in periodically, you'll want to be sure you get enough critical information from your business to be confident that it's healthy and crisis-free, and ensure that you can enjoy your time away.

The data you'll need will vary depending on your business, but here are a few examples of reports you should have completely standardized—you should get them at precise intervals (day/week/month—whatever works best for your business), and they should look the same every single time:

- Sales
- Cash flow
- New business and sales projections
- Profit/Loss

Contingency Systems

Every business owner knows that no two days are identical. Things happen. Disasters, big and small, appear out of nowhere. Changes in the market such as competition, legislation, pricing, availability of materials, and consumer trends can change the playing field for a given business very quickly.

Contingency systems are a best-attempt to define what should happen during such notable changes in business operations or market space.

The best way to develop a good contingency plan is to sit down with your staff and play a good round of 'what if'. You'll find your team well-equipped to brainstorm any number of scenarios that might leave them handicapped in your absence; they've probably been worrying about it for some time.

Some examples:

- What about an unusually large and unexpected expense? How will you handle money and signing authority?
- If your business is highly dependant on one or two large clients, what happens if one of those clients is slipping away?
- Under what circumstances can your staff contact you, and how will they do it?
- If key personnel need to be replaced in your absence, who will recruit a replacement? Do you need to return home to do it?

Get it All On Paper

When you boil it down, what you and your staff do on a day-to-day basis is usually a series of repeatable steps—a process. While some things are difficult to capture in a process—bedside manner, for example—much of daily operations can be distilled and written down.

Capturing all systems on paper creates an operational manual for use in your absence. It also pays permanent dividends: getting everything standardized will make your life a great deal easier after your sabbatical, too.

You'll also find that staff who are best suited for process-driven work—repetitive administrative tasks, for example—will appreciate a clear system for doing their job. They'll perform better, and as a result so will your business.

Step Three: People

All the systems in the world won't be much help if you still have to do all the work yourself. To truly escape, you'll need to replace the most complicated part in the business system: *you*.

Don't be skeptical. Every business with more than one employee has, to at least a limited extent, managed to turn part of their operations over to someone else. The larger and more successful the company, the more times they've done it. How else do uber-entrepreneurs like Bill Gates, Michael Dell and scores of others get from garages, basements and dorm rooms to enormous corporations with thousands of employees? They regularly replace themselves with other people so they can concentrate on what's important. In this case, what's important is getting you the break you want.

Step three is about taking all the things you identify as "your job" in your systems work in step two and finding someone else besides *you* to do them. There are three options for downloading your work to someone else: assign the work to existing people in your organization, add additional people, or replace underperforming people with staff that can do their original job plus take on additional responsibility.

It's important to remember that you're not just transferring responsibility to someone new—you'll need to transfer *authority*, too. There's nothing worse for an employee than being responsible, but not being allowed to make the decisions required to live up to that responsibility. If you can't trust your people, you've either got the wrong people, or you need to learn to trust. Either way, you'll have to resolve the issue.

Transferring authority means you'll have to allow your people to make decisions *and* mistakes. It also means you'll have to trust someone with the "keys to the castle"—you won't be able to manage the finances while you're away. If your business is small, and you handle this stuff yourself, someone's going to need signing authority up to a certain limit on your bank account.

Do you need to replace yourself with another person? That depends. Someone will likely have to do a lot of what you used to do, but does that mean you need to hire a new president to run the show? Will your current position continue to exist? Not necessarily. You'll be surprised at how well your existing staff can rise to the challenge of additional responsibility. However, depending on your business, you may need to fill your shoes with a paid employee.

No matter what your business is, though, it won't let you leave, until you leave it.

Step Four: Practice

Like all good escapes, leaving your business requires a few dress rehearsals. There are two types of "practicing" that you'll do before you leave.

Practice 1: A *Real* Vacation

When was the last time you took two weeks off, with absolutely no contact with your business? If you haven't done this in the last 12 months, than your first step here is to book yourself a holiday. Schedule two weeks off for as soon as you can. Put it in the calendar, and start planning for it.

Most small business owners don't take *any* vacation. Guess what? *You're not like that anymore.* As of right now, you're turning over a new leaf.

Taking a short vacation between now and your sabbatical time is critical. It helps you:

- Learn to be away, and to let go.
- Get your team accustomed to your absence.
- Find kinks in the system early on, and deal with problems that arise.

This "mini-sabbatical" is going to make the real thing a *lot* easier. If you don't have any experience with true vacations, a couple of weeks will make your longer hiatus a much more rewarding experience.

The secret here is to just book it. Once it's in the calendar at home and at the office, it's far more likely to happen. *Get the sequence right: book it first, figure it out later.*

Practice 2: Pre-Departure Trial

The best way to iron out the kinks of the no-you business is to...well, leave. Do a test run before you go. Some time before you leave, turn off your cell phone, and see how things go. You'll be surprised at how many kinks you'll work out in a week.

While there's clearly a practical side to this, there's also a huge emotional benefit to a trial run, particularly if you're leaving the country. Traveling or relocating can be stressful enough without wondering how things are working at home. A trial run is the best stress-reliever there is. Most of the kinks are little things that are easy to fix while you're in the office, but far more emotionally draining when you're halfway around the world. In our case, the trial run made a huge difference during the week or two it took to get email access and a phone.

What the pre-departure trial really means is that you start your sabbatical a week or two before you actually *leave*. The difference is that your staff *can* contact you if they need to, and you can come in to the office periodically to debrief on successes and challenges during the trial.

Strategies for Successfully Leaving Your Business

Keep an Open Mind

The biggest thing we've learned so far is to abandon your preconceived notions of what it means to leave your business. Thinking in terms of "losing as little money as possible while I'm away", or "maybe breaking even" are sure ways to do *exactly* that.

It may seem impossible but you *can* make money while on sabbatical. In fact, you can make *more* money on sabbatical than you do at work.

Leaving your business running without you there forces you to find other ways to generate revenue without simply selling your time, or doing all the work yourself. You'll be surprised at what you can accomplish—and how much you can earn—when you *have* to.

In planning for your time off, ask yourself questions like, "How could I make more money without being at my office than I could while I'm there?" If you allow yourself to freely brainstorm without judging, you'll be surprised at what you'll come up with.

Stay Big Picture

From 40,000 feet, the big picture of leaving your business (assuming you don't shut your doors) looks like this: clients consume products and services, and happily pay. It's a system for exchanging products or services for money. In the past, you may have been the main engine of that service, but now it's time to pass the torch.

Certainly leaving your business for any length of time—even a short vacation—can result in the world's longest to-do list. Resist the temptation, though, to get caught up in the details. Yes, they'll all have to be taken care of, but not at one time. Start a list right away, and just jot down all the little things as you go so you don't have to think about them until it's time.

While you're away, continue to focus on the larger picture. One slow day at the office doesn't mean your business is going down the tubes—each day's going to be a little different. Remember that you have slower days when *you're* there, too—one bad day doesn't make a trend. Micro-management isn't going to work when you're gone.

Embrace the Advantage of Long-Term Absence

"How can I take a year off if I can't even take a week?"

-Business owner

This is the big mental hurdle for most business owners. Looking back at the last few years, they realize that they were fortunate if they could take a week off never mind a *year*. How can they possibly do it?

The answer lies in the fact that vacations and sabbaticals are not the same creatures. They have different math, different intentions and different results.

In *Six Months Off*, the authors reveal what serial sabbaticalists know to be true. "One of the great secrets of a sabbatical," they point out, "is that taking more time off is easier than taking *less* time."[15]

You must be joking? How can that be?

It's true. Short term vacations are like undersized vehicles. You're asking too much of too little. When you take two weeks off, you work like crazy beforehand, you work like crazy after. In between, your staff and colleagues work like crazy. Perhaps even your clients have to sacrifice and accommodate, too. It's like taking six of your friends on a trip in your two-door compact car. It's simply not enough vehicle, but you can make it work for the short haul. For a long trip, it's not going to cut it.

However, if you had to take six people on a 6 *month* road trip, you'd do things differently. You'd get a large passenger van, maybe an RV. You'd make a system for trading drivers, sharing groceries, and splitting gas costs. You discover that you have more space, money, time and health in the RV than you *ever* did driving your compact two-door!

The same applies to your business. Taking *extended* time away forces you to move from coping to actually building systems that function without you.

Consider That it's not Supposed to Be Easy

Leaving your business is hard. It's a whole new skill set. For most entrepreneurs, what's really going on is a transition from owning a job to truly running a business, and that's a tough change. Don't expect it to be simple, but at the same time, don't expect it to be impossible or painful. Just expect it to be a challenge that you're well equipped for.

Accept the Worst-Case Scenario

Calculate the worst possible financial outcome for your business in your absence. What's a reasonable worst-case scenario? The purpose of this is to be able to say, "the worst thing that can happen is I'll lose $X, and I can live with that," and then get on with your planning. In reality, your clients *will* show up. The worst-case scenario is just that: worst-case, and it lies in the very fringes of probability. It just ain't gonna happen.

Ask yourself, "is it worth $X to be home with my new baby/travel/do volunteer work/etc.?" If the answer is yes, then move on.

Focus on What's Real

Once you've accepted the worst possible outcome, focus on what's real. Don't speculate on problems that aren't there (and likely won't be). Feel free to do a little disaster planning—data backups, staff changes, illness, fire, etc.—but don't obsess on issues that don't exist.

Obsessing over the *possibility* of declining revenue is not productive. *If* that happens, start generating positive solutions to the situation, but not until then. Learn to understand the difference between brainstorming solutions to possible outcomes, and obsessing over problems.

Give Up Your Ego

Small businesses tend to operate in an "owner is everything" environment. You may be used to doing everything yourself. Over time, that can evolve into believing you *have* to do everything yourself. That in turn, evolves into believing you're the only one who *can* do the job at all.

Let it go. The truth is that we're all dispensable. What's led you to believing that no one else can do your job is the unconscious feeling that no one else *cares* about your business as much as you. Instead of focusing on how no one else can do it, focus on finding ways to motivate your staff to care as much as you do.

Trust

Closely related to giving up your ego is *trust*. You must learn to trust other people to operate your business in your absence. You can't escape without it. Yes, there will be mistakes, but that's how you learn. And if you've managed to give up your ego, you'll know that *you* made many mistakes on the way, too. And look how well you turned out.

Make Time Your Ally

Start early. Take the time to find the right people and develop the systems and processes for them to do the same quality job every time. Starting early gives you a few key advantages. First, you can tweak and redevelop systems several times before you go, so that they operate smoothly in your absence. Second, you don't have to hire the first person you come across for a given job.

ᴄꙅ

Leaving a business is a bit like letting go of a child. It can be challenging, and it doesn't always go as planned, but in the end, it's best for your baby.

Sabbaticals have a special impact on business owners. While many employees return to their jobs after their hiatus, and slowly drift back to the rat race, the changes you make to your business in order to get away can pay dividends for a lifetime. Those changes can create a healthy work-life balance that you might never have achieved otherwise.

Every business is different. Yours is unique, and the steps you need to take to escape will be unique, too. Just remember that every business owner who successfully left their business did it because they *chose* to.

Don't be fooled into thinking you can't leave your baby. For every business owner who says they can't leave their business, there's another business in the same industry, that operates the same way, that is profitable, whose owner is watching the waves break on a pristine beach somewhere.

ESCAPING WITH CHILDREN

Don't limit a child to your own learning, for he was born in another time.

-Rabbinical saying

I WAS A LITTLE freaked out. After nearly 36 hours of travel, we were finally nearing our sabbatical destination. Five years of planning had culminated in a jarring drive down a precarious dirt road bordered by sugarcane fields and coco trees.

We had arrived in South America.

As we looked out the windows of the van, eager to catch a glimpse of what would become our home for the next five months, I glanced nervously over at our daughter.

Late the night before we had pushed Eve, our five year-old, through Paraguayan customs on a luggage cart. After a long flight, she was exhausted, and had curled up and fallen asleep on our suitcases.

The trip was tiring, but she was amazing. She exceeded our expectations every step of the way, and just her presence alone made things easier, as customs officials first in Brazil, then Paraguay, pulled us to the front of long lineups, smiling brightly at the precocious little girl in her pajamas clutching a stuffed yellow duck.

Still, despite Eve's super-traveler status and my calm demeanor, I was seriously nervous on the inside. *What were we thinking?* I thought. *This is crazy, bringing a kid here. We have no idea what we're getting into.*

To a large extent this was true. We'd agreed to come to Paraguay, a relatively low profile country in South America, over *coffee*. It was as simple as that. We weren't really sure exactly how things were going to be, but we knew that there were kids for Eve to play with, and I knew that I trusted (for no identifiable reason) the missionary who'd invited us.

Now, though, our "gut instinct" decision to come seemed ill-considered. This wasn't like our other sabbaticals, traveling alone or as a couple. We had a kid! If this went poorly, the consequences would be far more painful.

The van turned onto a beautiful property just as the sun set, and we approached a brick home in the distance. Eve looked at me. "Where are all the kids, daddy?"

"I don't know, sweetie. I'm sure they're here somewhere."

Moments later, as the van came to a stop, more than a dozen beautiful children appeared from nowhere, smiling, cheering, and shouting happily in Spanish. We emerged from the van, and were swarmed with hugs and warm welcomes. Eve looked at me, astonished, and then began to laugh with joy at the happy chaos.

Within minutes, little Eve, without a word of Spanish, was off happily playing.

The tension flooded out of me. *It's going to be fine*, I thought. *It's going to be great!*

And it was.

છ

For many families, there's a convergence point on the timeline of life where children and careers collide. The addition of kids to the existing stresses of work and modern culture can be overwhelming for many families. In fact, many don't make it.

In their book *The Two-Income Trap: Why Middle-Class Mothers and Fathers are Going Broke*, authors Elizabeth Warren and Amelia Warren Tyagi reveal the debilitating cycle for middle-class parents who buy into neighborhoods they can't afford in order to provide access to good schools for their children. The homes cost more, the taxes are higher, and the requisite level of accessories climbs as well. The only way to make ends meet is for both parents to work full time (at least).[16]

Furthermore, as more and more couples have children later in life, prime earning years have begun to overlap with prime rearing years, resulting in a whole new level of rat race intensity. Nights with less sleep are followed (far too quickly) by earlier mornings that have all the soothing tranquility of an air raid. The easy days are the ones that you can simply skip lunch and overwork yourself without having to pick up a sick child from school, hit a soccer game or make an orthodontist appointment you can't afford.

It's absolutely the last time anyone would dream of taking a sabbatical.

But it's also one of the best times to do it. The benefits for families taking sabbaticals are endless; they can build character, health, relationships and values in a way that's very difficult to achieve by any other means.

Like the other barriers to your hiatus, though, the sabbatical rock of children is a tough one to get rolling, and highly emotionally charged. In an effort to shift the boulder a bit, let's challenge the status quo on the biggest concerns about taking children on sabbatical: their safety, their schooling and your sanity.

Concern #1: Safety

Is it safe to take your kids on sabbatical? The answer is another question: what does safe mean? Safe is a term that really means, "a level of risk that I'm comfortable with".

Different sabbaticals have different levels of risk. Moving your family from Miami to San Diego for a sabbatical is more of a logistical challenge than a safety issue. New school, new friends, new house.

If you're considering a sabbatical with kids in a Second or Third World country, however, you're undoubtedly already worried about safety and access to adequate health care. For most people, other countries mean "more risk".

Worrying about your kids is easy. It's *normal*–every good parent wants their child to be safe and well. What's not healthy is worrying yourself sick about it. And what's not so easy is assessing the *real* risk in other countries while you're still sitting at home in First World comfort.

This is not an attempt to convince you there is no risk—it's a suggestion that you carefully consider the context of the information you receive, and how it fits with your sabbatical plans. Consider what follows as a set of discussion points to review *before* you discount traveling with children because of safety concerns.

Danger is a Squeaky Wheel

Bad news, drama, danger and catastrophe make news. Your main sources of information on another country will tend to come from sources that have a vested interest in reporting the unpleasant side of life. Vaccine producers, newspapers, websites, doctors and even your friends and family will have plenty to say about crime, communicable disease and natural disaster. They'll have far less to say about families who forged new bonds and created lasting memories during Second and Third world travel.

This isn't to say that these sources are all nasty. It's simply how the world works. If danger *wasn't* a squeaky wheel, a lot more of us would fall victim to it. Focusing on threats is a built-in survival mechanism, and it works wonders for keeping us alive.

At times, however, it also works wonders for keeping us in our homes in front of televisions (watching more unpleasant news) instead of exploring the world. The trick is to recognize that you're only seeing one side of the story. You're not hearing about the enormous percentage of people leading safe and happy lives. You're not hearing about them because *they don't make the news.*

Seeking Safety and Dodging Danger Are Not The Same

Ironically, when you go searching for information on *safety* in another country, you actually tend to search for information on *danger*. We don't, for example, tend to look for infant *immortality* rates, we look for mortality rates. We don't ask how many people *didn't* get malaria. The same goes for crime. It takes only a few minutes on the internet to find the number of murders in a given country—it's a lot harder to find the number of people who *didn't* die. I challenge you to find the statistics for the number of *non*-victims of crime, disease and natural disaster for any country—the stats don't exist, yet the non-victims outnumber the victims many times over.

The result is that the information we get is almost entirely negative, because that's what we're *looking* for.

Your Circumstances Are Not the Same

When you leave the First World for the Third, you're not becoming a Third World person. Your existing level of health, your access to resources and your background and education provide you and your family with an enormous advantage over many inhabitants of less developed nations. You can afford health care. You can afford good food. You can afford clean water. You can afford decent housing. The same statistics don't apply to you.

Take the time to consider the whole picture before you discount a sabbatical because it's too dangerous for children.

Concern #2: School

Face it: North America hasn't cornered the market on schools. Schooling options are plentiful around the world. You can home school, if that suits you, or put your children in a local school. Many countries have English-speaking private schools for expatriates that tend to be expensive, but of good quality.

Remember that *education* doesn't have to mean sitting at a desk, either. By discussing your time away with teachers and school administrators, you may be able to use your travel as a form of education in itself. What sounds more educational to you: reading a textbook in class about indigenous South American people, or hiking to Machu Picchu to see the Incan ruins first hand? Which experience do you think has the most staying power?

The trick to getting comfortable with alternative forms of education is to get educated. Talk to teachers, parents and your kids about how they feel. And remember that little kids are...well, they're little kids. Your preschooler isn't going to suffer if they miss a standardized test or fall behind in reading for the time you're away. Give your little ones a chance to be little ones.

Concern #3: Staying Sane

Although modern living can be crushingly difficult at times, it also contains an entire infrastructure of sanity-preserving resources that have evolved around the need to integrate child rearing with income earning.

The school system, daycare, sports teams, nannies, television, video games, playgrounds and DVD's all provide a cushion between our insanely busy lives, and the wondrous but demanding exuberance of kids. And regardless of your opinion of these safety valves, it's worth considering what your sabbatical will be like *without* them.

The average kid watches several hours of TV per day. If that's not part of your sabbatical, what will your day be like? I'm not suggesting it'll be better or worse, only that it will be different, and it's worth envisioning what that "different" will be like, and how you'll deal with it.

What Kids Really Need

If the thought of going from Nintendo to none-tendo sends you into a panic attack, consider for a moment what kids *actually* need to be fulfilled and happy.

You

Although it may not be easy to believe, particularly with teenagers, your kids really want you. What they lose in DVD releases on sabbatical, they make up for with pure, unfettered time with *you*. Your time away can easily create and strengthen bonds with your children that will last a lifetime—all it takes is a little time.

Other Kids

Kids are social creatures, and just like parents need adult time, kids need kid time—they need to interact with other children.

Our daughter is an only child. For this reason, we chose a destination for our most recent sabbatical that would have many other children around. It was the smartest thing we could have done. From the moment we arrived, the children took Eve under their wing, and despite the language barrier, had an incredible time.

The message is a simple one: kids are kids, all around the world. If you've got an only child, or kids of diverse ages, or siblings that don't get along, don't worry. Find a place with kids, and the kids will find their place.

(Some) Structure

Children tend to gravitate towards some structure. Rules and routine are a way for them to test the world out, and figure out how things work. Just as touching a hot stove equals pain for a toddler, staying out late without calling home equals disapproval for a teenager. They're all forms of poking and prodding the world to find out how it will respond.

Too much structure can be stifling. Too little can be unrewarding, or even scary.

How does this apply to sabbaticals? Most families transitioning from rat race to sabbatical life may find themselves moving from too much structure and routine to too little. It can make for a difficult transition.

Recognize that while you may relish the idea of having absolutely *zero* rules, restrictions and obligations when you wake up on the first day of your sabbatical, your children may feel otherwise. Keep them informed and involved. Even if there are no plans whatsoever, tell them, "The plan is to have no plan so we can just relax and enjoy ourselves today."

Good Intentions

Unlike many adults, children are remarkably intuitive. Babies know far better than adults when they're hungry. Toddlers know exactly what they want (even if they can't get it), and even moody, confused teenagers have a remarkable ability to gravitate towards what they like. We grown-ups, on the other hand, have had the pleasure of being completely desensitized by the incredible world that's evolved around us—a lot of our intuition lies dormant.

The result is that kids are sensitive to the environment around them. They have a natural ability to pick up on emotions and intentions. For this reason, one of the best tools for travel with children is your *attitude* for travel with children. If you tell yourself that a 12-hour flight is going to be rough with your kids, then it's almost a sure thing.

Your kids will pick up on the subtle signals you send out—your body cues, your emotional tone, and your choice of language. Conversely, tell yourself that the cross-country RV trip is going to be fantastic, and it will be. Kids are the shortest route to self-fulfilling prophecy on the planet.

The Perfect Age is Any Age

What's the secret to choosing the right age? *Don't discount any ages.* Just as there's no perfect time to take your sabbatical, there's no perfect age for kids either. It's going to be great at any age. Don't assume your toddler is too young, or your teen too old. Young children provide an opportunity to skew the decision-making towards what you'd like to do, which tends to make things easy, but older kids represent a communal planning opportunity that can't be beat.

Sabbaticals and kids go together like peanut butter and jelly. The natural curiosity of kids, their desire to *engage* with life can take you to places and things you might never have dreamed of on your own.

Do your children a favor. Don't wait until they're gone.

THE FOOLPROOF THREE-STEP ESCAPE PLAN

I KNOW WHAT YOU'RE thinking. *This stuff all sounds good, but it just ain't gonna happen.*

You've likely tried something in the past and failed. Something big, like losing weight, quitting smoking, exercising regularly, changing jobs, or eating better. And they're tough, believe me. If you failed at any of those, consider yourself in good company.

But don't let your past experience poison you. This seemingly complete uprooting of your life is actually a lot easier than that other hard stuff.

But I also know that what you're thinking is dangerously close to true. It's just so easy to *not* go. What's crazy, though, is that the difference between leaving and staying hinges on such a few tiny little things. Simple stuff. The kind that can be sorted out in a few minutes over coffee. Really—once you get those big rocks rolling, it's just not that hard.

Over time, we've found that three simple little actions can make the difference between dreaming and departing. So here's the drill. Starting RIGHT NOW, do the following. Don't wait—these are all practical steps that can be done in a few minutes:

1. **Start the automatic savings plan outlined in the money chapter.** Do it online if you have internet banking, but if not, call your bank *right now* and get it done. At least make the appointment to see your banker if that's your only option.

2. **Choose a departure date and duration, and book it** in all home and work calendars. (You'll be able to tweak this later—the important thing is to block off the time.)

3. **Tell four people about your sabbatical plans**, at least one of
    which is a key decision-maker at work.

I'm not kidding. Three steps. Just do them now, and then figure
out the rest as you go. That's all you need.

Sound crazy? The magic in those three simple steps is it creates *momentum*. It gets you started. And getting started has the wonderful effect
of activating the four secrets; on top of the commitment these steps
represent, you'll also find your desire is kindled, you begin to envision
your sabbatical in even more detail then ever, and, perhaps for the first
time, you start to truly believe you can pull this off after all.

Because it's true. You can.

Pitfalls, Fears and Excuses

HE FOUR SECRETS ARE powerful tools. With them, and a little
organization, even the most entrenched rat-racer can escape the
relentless tug of the tides of life and find a dream sabbatical.

Even the best-laid plans, though, are subject to change. Not
everything can be measured, predicted and accounted for, and escape
planning is particularly susceptible to shifts in attitude and circum-
stance. From bad luck to bad decisions, these shifts are potential pitfalls
that can derail the most dedicated dreamer—to disregard them would be
folly.

The best way to deal with potential pitfalls is to mentally prepare
for them before they happen. Not in the sense of pessimistic nay-saying,
but in a productive, positive way. As you read through each of these,
consider them from a place of *solutions*: "If this occurs in my life, how
will I deal with it to ensure that it doesn't derail me from my plans?"

Waiting

Here's the sure-fire quickest way to remove all the stress, anxiety,
work and cost from your escape: *don't go*.

Don't go, but *tell* yourself that you'll go "later". It'll work wonders
for your stress. You'll never actually take a sabbatical, of course, but
things will be much easier.

The problem is that many people—yourself included—really *want* to take time away. Faced with the dilemma of wanting something badly, but being unable to deal with the associated anxiety, we resort to an easy solution that lets us sleep easy: we wait.

And each day we wait, we tell ourselves a story. *I'll wait until I retire. We'll go when the kids are older. When I have the money, then I can do it. We can do it when we're not so busy. Maybe after my next promotion, when things quiet down a bit.*

Each story buys us a little extra peace of mind, a little more time without emotional discord.

A sabbatical is the easiest thing in the world to NOT do. The problem is that nothing kills dreams faster than waiting.

Stephen Covey, author of *The Seven Habits of Highly Successful People*, has an enlightening approach to how we prioritize things in our life. Consider that everything you do in a day can be ranked on two scales: its *urgency*, and its *importance*. The trick is to realize that urgent things—returning phone calls, checking email, and putting out figurative fires aren't always important. They're just *loud*. The urgent things in our lives tend to be like the squeaky wheel—they get all the attention. But the important things—planning for your future, time with loved ones, taking care of your health—they're "outsqueaked" by the urgent things.

The result is that day after day, we put off what is important until tomorrow. Then we do it again, and again, and eventually, tomorrow is the last day there is. At that point, everything important that we delayed gets put in a new category.

That category is called *regret*. It's a nasty spot.

So how do you avoid waiting? Return to the fourth secret: commitment. If you tend to put things off, find a way to commit that locks you in. Find a small action that gives you big leverage. For example, buying a plane ticket only takes a few minutes, but it could be the commitment that gives you six months of freedom. Small action, big leverage.

Financial

Financial concerns are normal, common, and practically inevitable. You're going to have some.

With that knowledge comes the solution: expect them, and accept them. Concern for your financial future while planning your exit is a good thing. It ensures that you're taking the proper steps to manage your resources and create a successful re-entry to regular life.

Concern is good. Financial *panic*, on the other hand, is not as helpful. How do you tell the difference? Financial *concern* manifests as intelligent action—you take real steps to protect, grow and manage your resources. Financial panic, on the other hand, doesn't lead to action. It leads to long, scary internal dialogues about wearing a burlap sack and eating out of a dumpster.

How can you deal with financial worries? Start by accepting that worry is normal and healthy. If you could walk away from your job without giving a second thought to money, than you probably wouldn't be reading this. **Anyone who's ever left their job or business for a long-term leave has worried about money.** Don't worry that you're worrying. A little concern is helpful. The secret is to put that concern to productive use. *Take action by following the steps in the chapter on money.* They'll work for you every time.

Sudden Change in Plans

Life has a way of changing things on us. This is usually done without asking our permission, too, although when we look back the hints are usually pretty obvious.

Don't expect this unexpectedness to change during the time leading up to your sabbatical. Sudden health problems, surprise expenses and work transitions tend to happen when you least expect them. The trick is to expect them. Don't dwell on them, just assume that there will be the odd roadblock in your way, and that you will simply drive over it or around it and continue on your way.

Criticism

Although sabbaticals are increasing in popularity, you're not going to be in the majority when you go from boardroom to beach bum.

You may experience some "critical commentary". Some of it will be gently wrapped in well-meaning questions like, "what about your job?" or "aren't you worried about your pension?", but it may feel like criticism all the same. Perceive this for what it is:

- Envy that you're doing something they'd like to.
- Sadness that you're leaving.

- Genuine concern for your well-being.
- An inability to really comprehend what you're doing.
- An inability to conceive that a sabbatical could be valuable or enjoyable.

Once you recognize where the criticism comes from, smile and forget about it. It's your life, you get one shot, and you're far better off firing the shot yourself than having someone else do it for you.

Fear/Worry/Anxiety

"Remembering that you are going to die is the best way I know to avoid the trap of thinking you have something to lose."

-Steve Jobs, CEO of Apple Computer
Stanford University Commencement address, 2005

I can tell you now that your sabbatical's going to flash by in an instant. I can reassure you that not long after you return, your life will be "normal" again and you'll wonder why you ever worried about all the stuff you worried about. I can tell you that just about everything that concerns you right now in planning your time away is of no consequence—it won't happen, or if it does, it won't be the big deal you think it is. In short, your sabbatical's going to be fantastic, and all the worry is a waste of time.

But that's not going to help. You'll need to discover for yourself that there was nothing to worry about. In the meantime, you're probably going to worry just the same. Fortunately, there's a way to deal with the anxiety that comes with planning your exit.

Anticipate it

Expect some anxiety. You're not buying bread, you're changing your life. That requires some initiative and effort, and those are often accompanied by worry. Even if you think you're calm, cool-headed and super-prepared, expect to wake up at least once in the middle of the night on the brink of a panic attack. It's normal.

Accept it

Once you know the worry is coming, you only have to accept one simple truth: you *will* be able to deal with the anxiety of making significant changes in your life. Period. Trust me, you will.

Isolate it

Unless you have a psychological condition, anxiety is usually related to something specific. Develop the habit of discovering *precisely* what's causing you anxiety. A good way to do this is to ask yourself, "If I could snap my fingers and instantly change one thing in my life to eliminate this worry, what would it be?" Make sure the answer is something specific, not a vague "cancel my sabbatical" solution.

Address it

Once you've found that one thing that's bothering you, take action. Brainstorm possible solutions, talk it out with someone. Find ways to move forward. Most of our worries never come to pass, and taking action generally accelerates the process of coming to terms with that.

Reluctant Participants

You're brimming with desire, empowered by belief, energized by your vision...but your spouse doesn't *want* to escape. What do you do then?

Spouses, kids and other stakeholders may not always share your sabbatical dreams. Their idea of "getting away from it all" may be quite different from yours—in fact, change may be the last thing in the world they want. Remember that they have lives, too—their own unique weave of friends, jobs, emotions, dreams and fears that make up day-to-day existence. And that individual tapestry might not be suited to hanging on the wall of your sabbatical castle.

What do you do when you experience resistance from a partner? There are three important things to remember: communicate, communicate, communicate. You cannot resolve these things without open discussion. Even with a *willing* partner, lack of communication is an escape killer. Talk it over, and repeat. And repeat.

Same Desire, Different Vision

The "easiest" type of reluctant partner is the one who already has a desire to get away, but isn't interested in eight months at the Antarctic research station that you've been salivating over. The process in this instance is really one of discovering whether you're willing to accommodate both visions within the same sabbatical, or sacrificing yours for theirs. Are you willing to give up your polar bears for your spouse's palm trees? If not, it might be unreasonable to expect the same in return.

Work through the process of creating a sabbatical vision for *each* of your dreams. You may be surprised to find common ground, a way to do both, or a side of your partner's dream that appeals to you in a way you never imagined.

Different Desire

Fortunately, the same individual heartprint that might make your getaway partner reluctant to embrace your sabbatical also gives them their own set of desires. Somewhere inside them is a want—the seed of desire—that can be nurtured into something bigger.

Can you discover that seed? Is there something in their desire that's a match for yours? Better still, can you embrace what *they* want? Can you help them pursue their dreams in the knowledge that yours will come to you?

Taking Turns

What if your partner isn't reluctant, but can't get away? While you might consider the option of taking turns, give it some thought first. Taking turns for individual sabbaticals is not the same thing as going together. It's a fantastic way to find new careers, discover passions and further education and skills, but it's not a sabbatical with your partner.

If your partner really wants to go, but *can't*, then your first step is to revisit the concept of Belief. Why do they feel they can't? What's holding them back?

A Note on Reluctant Kids

While twenty years at the grindstone may have left you bursting with desire to get away from it all, you might find that children, depending on their ages, can be far from enthused at the thought of leaving behind *their* world. Can you blame them? Relatively speaking, they just got here. Their party's just started.

Don't ignore their concerns. Remember that although your kids might not have the decision-making clout to derail a sabbatical, they most certainly have the power to seriously curtail your enjoyment of it. Hear what they have to say. Ask questions, and try to understand their point of view. Remember that you were a teenager once, way, way back before the rat race wore you out—would you have wanted to leave your friends behind?

Take the time to share your vision, and hear their story. Be willing to find a common ground—is there a part of your vision that they can get excited about? Are you willing to change your plans to accommodate theirs?

If you're traveling with kids, consider making them active participants in the planning and decision-making. Let them know that you'll make the final decisions, but that you'd like to hear everything they have to say.

Doubt

All of the various concerns, fears, anxieties and worries that circulate during your sabbatical tend to plant seeds for one big-ass tree of *doubt*. When you go against the norm, you may find yourself questioning your decision. This, too, is normal.

Stay the course. The rewards of your time away will come, and they'll be more than you imagine. Stick to your plan, and have confidence in your decision.

CB

What's important throughout the time leading up to your time away is this: don't let anxieties, roadblocks and unexpected events cast a shadow on your decision to go. *Worry does not mean your sabbatical is a bad idea.* Trust your desire to leave. If you want it, it's the right thing for you.

PART 3: Doing It

If there were in the world today any large number of people who desired their own happiness more than they desired the unhappiness of others, we could have paradise in a few years.

-Bertrand Russell

GETTING THE MOST OUT OF YOUR ESCAPE

S EVERAL YEARS AGO I took a long road trip with some good friends. We had a few days of highway travel ahead of us, so we got serious and planned the essentials. The music, refreshments, snacks, itinerary, map and even personalized shirts were all prepared in advance. Each person planned to take shifts at the wheel, and we calculated how long it would take to reach our destination based on highway speeds and periodic rest stops. Every detail was accounted for.

Twenty minutes into the trip, the co-pilot *threw the map out the window*.

There were a few moments of shocked silence. Then chaos erupted. Littering aside, we were appalled—how were we supposed to get where we were going without a map? How would we know where to turn? What would we do? And more importantly, why? *Why, why, why?*

"No maps allowed," was all he would say.

With our "no map" restriction firmly in place, we took wrong turns, got lost, asked directions, stopped to scratch our heads and look around, and generally had the best road trip that anyone could ever ask for. We even arrived (almost) on time. We had a purpose, but no plan. We had a mission, but no map.

We had the time of our lives.

I learned a lot from our renegade co-pilot that day. A plan is a plan—that's all. It's a tool to help you shape what you think your time away should look like, and to make sure you have the resources—tangible and emotional—that you'll need to make it a success.

Like this book, *your plan is a guidebook, not a rulebook.* You don't have to follow it. Moreover, you can throw it out the window anytime you like. (Although please don't litter.)

That being said, here are some suggested ways to improve your sabbatical experience. After all, you've worked hard to get here. You should squeeze every drop of joy you can from it.

Become a Yes Person

A common side effect of years of rat race entrenchment is a magnetic attraction to "no". Stress, anxiety and overloaded schedules change our default position from positive to negative—when opportunities present themselves, our knee-jerk response is to think, *No—that'll be too much work. I've got enough on my plate.*

It takes time to realize that your sabbatical plate may be far roomier than your previous one. And it takes even more time still to rewire your brain to start welcoming change and opportunity into your life. But if you can, make a conscious decision to default to "yes". Try new things. Go to new places. Make new friends. Get out of the house.

This doesn't mean you should jam your schedule solid all over again. Just know that all of the great memories created in your sabbatical will start with the simple word *yes*. You just have to use it.

Trust

The best sabbaticals are taken with a dose of faith. Learn to trust that things will work out—after all, they almost always do, and there's no return on thinking otherwise.

Learn to trust others, too. If you're in a new culture, remember that people are people. Be smart, but have some faith in good human nature. Why think otherwise? Obsessing over theft and violence is only likely to bring you into contact with it—you'll spend half your time away seeing evidence of it in the papers, on the TV, and in the streets because *that's what you'll be looking for*. Try focusing on the positive, and you'll discover that there's so much of it that you won't have time for the negative. Be smart, not paranoid.

Take Your Time

Everything's arranged. The boss is onboard, the house is rented, your stuff is in storage—it's time to put the pedal down, right?

Wrong. You've got six months. Take your time. When was the last time you had this much time to *not* rush? You've got weeks and weeks of unscheduled time—resist the urge to program all of it. Sure you don't want to squander it, but at the same time, do you really want to be in a hurry? Isn't that part of the idea—to escape that kind of constant running?

Besides, the hurrying doesn't generally produce much return. How many times have you been in bumper-to-bumper traffic, and watched someone weaving in and out of every hole, nosing into every gap, changing lanes at every opportunity? Five minutes later, they're right beside you again, still struggling. The reality is that *hurry doesn't pay well*, and your time away is the perfect time to test the hypothesis. Take your time. Smell the roses, as they say.

Roll With the Punches

When you exit the rat race, you're not just leaving a job. You're leaving an intricate system that you've created over the years to manage your life. It's a complex and remarkable set of coping processes that lets you navigate traffic, get the kids to school, arrive at work on time, keep your head above water and make it home in time to eat and get to soccer.

In the absence of this structure—say, on a six month backpacking adventure though Africa—stuff happens. Things become less predictable. Routine is disrupted. You may be unable to plan everything. Events fly out of left field and leave you a bit stunned.

But for every ounce of these disconcerting events, there are a hundred pounds of joy. Learning to go with the flow during your time off will lead you to far less stress, and far more happiness than you can imagine. When your sabbatical throws you a curve, accept it as part of the experience—and remember some of your best stories and memories are going to come from those unexpected events.

Acculturize

In days of yore, international travelers needed to make dramatic changes in their lives in order to function. Eating local food and learning the language were near-necessities for survival.

Now, you can travel to almost any country in the world, speak only English, and sleep in a comfortable bed every night. You can eat meals in Americanized restaurants where the food tastes almost the same as home—you can choose French fries over fried beetles anytime.

In short, you can travel the world without ever *experiencing* it.

But is that really what you want? After all, we're talking about escape—if you really want things to be the same, it's a lot easier to just stay home, isn't it?

Embracing a "when-in-Rome" attitude while on sabbatical will create some of your most memorable moments. Adopting local customs, learning the language (even a little bit) and trying the food will not only broaden your experience, but you'll find that most cultures are far more open to the people who are open to culture. It's a positive feedback loop—trying more things gives you more opportunity to try more things.

Learn Something...

Henry Ford once said "Anyone who stops learning is old, whether at twenty or eighty." While I can't vouch for the principle, I can testify to its inverse: *learning keeps you young*. It *youthens*, for lack of a better word.

This goes hand in hand with becoming a 'yes' person. Rise to the challenge of trying something new, you'll find your mind and body soaking up new skills like a sponge.

...and Unlearn Something

Almost as if he anticipated Ford's persistent trek towards standardization, Mark Twain put it quite differently: "Education consists mainly of what we have unlearned."

It wouldn't be unreasonable to describe modern life as a collection of sequenced habits. Get up. Make coffee. Shower. Drive to work.

Come home. Cook dinner. While there's no need to abandon shower-ing for your entire hiatus, there may be some other things worth unlearning during your time away.

Between the lines of the physical habits of daily life, a subtext of *emotional* habits guides our thinking from moment to moment. We're stressed by traffic during our commute. We're anxious about an important meeting that afternoon. Frustrated by a botched conversa-tion with a spouse. And as the emotions associated with physical habits become habitual themselves, our outlook slowly shifts: pessimism and negativity begin to become default world views, and our rose-colored glasses slowly discolor.

Sometimes this shift is so subtle it's impossible to notice without a new frame of reference. Your sabbatical is that new vantage point. And once you notice the view is different, take Twain's advice and unlearn some habits that no longer serve you.

Rough It

Even if you've got the cash to live it up the whole time you're gone (In which case, what are you waiting for? You could be reading this on the plane), it's worth giving budget life a shot. First class is great, but you'll get a *different* experience by trying things in economy.

Connect With Others

The image of your sabbatical in your mind's eye likely involves two things: a place and an activity. Reading a great novel in a hammock. Hiking the Himalayas. Exploring the architecture of Rome. Working on your poetry in a cheap apartment in San Francisco. Providing medical care to the needy in Africa.

The reality is that your time away is very likely to involve new *people*, too. Changing your location and your daily habits is almost guaranteed to bring you into contact with many new faces, and the more you shake up the geography and the routine, the more new faces you'll find.

With all these people around, it behooves you to *talk* to some of them. If that makes you want to slam this book shut right now, fear not—this isn't about becoming an extroverted mover and shaker. It's a gentle reminder that in the long run, life tends to be about relation-ships, not architecture.

If you're actively traveling, you'll find other travelers more than willing to talk. They may seem aloof at first, but it's usually just shyness. Almost everyone opens up when approached.

Do Some Nothing

In his bestseller *In Praise of Slow: How a Worldwide Movement is Challenging the Cult of Speed*, Carl Honoré describes his inability to slow down and do nothing:

> *"At the gate, I join the back end of a long lineup, where there is nothing to do except, well, nothing. Only I am no longer capable of doing nothing."*

Skimming a newspaper, Honoré stumbles across what might just be the ultimate symbol of speed obsession: "One Minute Bedtime Stories"–classic fairy tales condensed into "sixty-second sound bites".

In the epiphany that would lead him to write In Praise of Slow, Honoré catches himself. "Have I gone insane?" he writes. "My whole life has turned into an exercise in hurry, in packing more and more into every hour."[17]

Of all the rat race woes, the most common seems to be the lost time to relax. "I just want to have some time to do nothing," is a prevalent cry. Yet, given the opportunity to do just that, we have a tendency to do the opposite. Our vacations (if we take them) are jam-packed with activities, side trips and scheduled events. Weekends are crammed full of social and sporting events.

There's more to this phenomenon than just busy schedules. Over-clocking our 24-7 week has two significant impacts on our lives that extend beyond the rat race "treadmill" feeling. The first is that busy schedules prevent us from giving serious consideration to the state of our lives. Whether this is head-in-the-sand behavior or simple bewilderment depends on the individual, but the outcome is the same: we don't have the contemplative headspace to back up and view our lives in the larger scheme of things. We're running so fast to keep from falling off the treadmill that we're unable to see it to begin with.

The second impact is that hectic scheduling becomes habitual. Given the opportunity for contemplative, unprogrammed time, we'll choose to schedule more things in that time because that's what we're used to doing. And habits are not only repetitive behavior, they're self-supporting; over time we come to believe that the habit is the *correct* behavior. *Not* doing something becomes Bad or Lazy.

What does this mean to your time off? It means you may have to make a specific effort to do nothing. To just be. Think a bit. Look around. Feel happy, or feel sad, but feel something. It may feel awkward, particularly at the start of your sabbatical, but give it a shot. The clarity that comes from deeper, unhurried examination of your life is well worth the hammock time.

CȜ

What's the real secret to getting the most from your time away? *The true secret to making the most of your escape is to make sure you go.*

You're going to be fine once you get moving. The only way you can really ruin your sabbatical is to never go.

COMING OUT AHEAD
Tips for Taking a Sabbatical Without Losing Ground

O N CLOSE INSPECTION, THE anxieties of taking a sabbatical are less about fear of air travel or concerns about safety issues while on leave, and more about losing what we have. In the end, we're scared of losing ground. Can you take a sabbatical without sacrificing career ground or business growth? Can your savings, investments and retirement timelines survive an extended leave? The answer is an unequivocal *yes*. In fact, you can prosper on all counts, coming out further ahead in the long run.

Strategies for Coming Out Ahead

Taking time off without losing ground is an inside job, too—it's mainly a mental game. Try some of these mental "recalibrations" to change your perception of the impact of your time away.

Move from Cost Thinking to Investment Thinking

The easiest way to ensure that you don't lose ground during your sabbatical is simply this: *change your mind*. Your sabbatical can only be a sacrifice if you choose to see it that way, so why not see it as an investment?

If that seems overly simplistic, consider the multitude of benefits your time away generates. You can improve your health, reconnect with loved ones, learn new skills, learn a language, train for a new career, find a new business opportunity, discover your passion, and raise your financial prowess. And that's just the tip of the iceberg.

Aren't these investments? Most people don't question spending tens of thousands of dollars on a car that loses value every day; what could be wrong with investing in your health or personal development?

What makes it difficult to see things this way is simply status quo thinking. We've been raised and programmed to believe that time on the job is what really matters. We occasionally pay lip service to "quality time", but the truth is that we don't really believe it. What we do believe is that work is good, relaxing is bad. Big company life is good, free-thinking is bad.

Change your mind. Move from thinking of the cost of your time away to the investment in your time away, and the dividends that investment will pay for your entire life.

Recalibrate Success: Beyond Money

It would be easy to measure the outcome of your sabbatical in terms of its financial impact. After all, that's the biggest concern most people have when leaving, so it seems only natural to use dollars as a yardstick for sabbatical success. Or as a measure of the "cost" of your sabbatical.

The problem with measuring in dollars is that it's extraordinarily difficult to put a price tag on many sabbatical benefits. What dollar value do you place on reconnecting with your spouse? What's the price of innumerable memories that you can hold for a lifetime? What's it worth to you to reclaim your health?

For these benefits (and they are many), we have to turn to our intuition. We know deep in our gut that there is no price tag for lifetime connection with our children—we just know it's worthwhile when it happens. We know we can't put a price on dodging that heart attack or stroke (unless you work for an insurance company, there's no barcode for "staying alive") we just know deep inside that the almighty dollar fails us as a yardstick.

Expand your definition of sabbatical success to include the intangibles and un-measurables. Resist the temptation to see only receipts and bills, checks and deposits.

In fact, here's what's *really* going to happen: you're going to be so astonished by the success of your time away that not only will you not have the faintest idea of *how* to put a price tag on all you've gained, but you'll know with absolute certainty that there's no point in doing so; you'll know your sabbatical has already paid for itself a thousand times over.

Recalibrate Time: Seeing a Longer Picture

What about the things you *can* put a price tag on? After all, it's not difficult to tally up all your expenses while you're away on one side of the page, and your income (if any) on the other side. That profit or loss is a very concrete number. The truth, however, is that it's not the whole picture.

What about the skills you learn while away that earn you higher pay? What about the changes in your confidence and determination that bring about your next promotion? What about the changes in your business that allow you to earn without being there? These types of changes pay dividends for your *whole life*, and no financial picture of success, then, is complete until it takes into account the raises, bonuses, better jobs and profits that come from your sabbatical learnings. And while you can argue that your promotion might have happened anyway, who's to say that these many financial blessings won't arrive much *sooner* than they would have otherwise? As anyone with a small amount of investment knowledge knows, time is extraordinarily important in compounding—a few thousand dollars this year as opposed to many years from now can make all the difference to your future net worth.

Pour A Third Cup (Don't burn bridges)

In some Asian cultures, when someone is to depart there's a practice of pouring an extra cup of tea at the table—one more than is required for the two people seated. The extra cup of tea is said to be for "next time"—it's a symbol of the intent to reconnect at some future point. The third cup is a way of saying "see you later", instead of goodbye.

Exiting the rat race requires many farewells—you'll be surprised not only by the number of colleagues, associates, friends and family you *have*, but by how many want to connect with you before you go. Consider making those farewells "see you laters" as opposed to "good-byes".

This is particularly important in work/business farewells. In the context of your professional life—your job, career, or business—think of the third cup as not burning any bridges. While many people fantasize about the day they can say "take this job and shove it", consider choosing a "take this job and *save* it" attitude. After all, you can burn a bridge in an instant, but it can take years to build one.

Your time away will pass faster than you think, and it's impossible to predict in advance your mindset, needs and desires when you return to your life. Pouring the third cup doesn't mean you have to drink it, anymore than leaving a bridge intact means you have to cross it. It simply leaves you with *options*.

Stay in touch

I once heard a story of a missionary who spent over 30 years working in China without ever asking for money. He simply followed his evangelical calling. He had no salary, or regular income, and he never begged or asked for money, but he always *had* money.

What was his secret? Every day the missionary wrote a letter. He never asked for anything, only described his work, his life, and passed on his prayers for others. In return, he received a steady stream of financial support for his work in China that allowed him to continue his efforts.

While this is a great example of the power of giving, it also has a more tangible message: stay in touch while you're away. Not because you expect people to send money for your sabbatical efforts (although they may well do so), but because sustaining relationships is important, and these days, it's also *easy*.

Our first sabbaticals were before the days of email, and I clearly remember the scramble to collect mailing addresses before leaving, and the countless hours spent beneath palm trees writing postcards and letters. Now, you can write one letter and personalize it for hundreds of people at the click of a button, and send it in a few seconds without the cost of even one stamp. Unless you intentionally choose not to, there's no real excuse for not staying in touch.

Besides, you might just inspire someone.

Become more valuable

One sure-fire way to return home to a higher point on the food chain is to improve yourself—to simply become more valuable while you're gone. Returning to the workplace or business environment with more skills and better self-understanding can only help your future success.

To some extent, this is almost an automatic function of taking extended time away. The sabbatical experience lends itself well to learning new "hard" skills like languages and technical abilities, as well as soft skills like decision-making, communication and problem solving. These are the skills most desired by the modern workplace, and most valuable to business owners.

And further still, exiting the rat race is a character builder. While anyone can take a sabbatical, those who actually *do* find increased self-reliance, confidence, and self-esteem. They all tend to rise when you step outside the status quo and do something for *yourself*.

Re-entry: Coming Home

A man travels the world over in search of what he needs and returns home to find it.

-George Moore

COMING HOME IS A subtle, joyful, but inevitably jarring experience that can leave you feeling more than a little disturbed. It's wonderful and terrible, relieving and disturbing, all at the same time. It's tough to describe.

The only way to understand coming home is to experience it, and you will. It'll be strange and uncomfortable, but you'll deal with it; if you can get away, you can most certainly come back.

Reentry isn't just about gathering up the threads of where you left off. Much as you may miss the habits and conveniences of your old life and, even look forward to having them back, you may also find them strangely unfamiliar. It's as if you've lost weight being away, and the things in your life that used to fit now hang loosely on you while you shamble around inside them.

Inevitably, though, you'll find your rhythm. Like riding a bike, it all comes back to you, sometimes with a speed that's frightening. Other times, it seems as if you'll *never* readjust. Here are some tips to manage (or avoid) those moments:

Leave a Little Breathing Room

If you've used your sabbatical to travel, especially to somewhere quite different, then leave yourself some time between returning home and starting work. You'll be glad you did. Give yourself a week to get your act together, unpack, and settle into the pace of your old life again.

Expect it to Be Harder than You Expect

It's normal to be excited to get back to your normal life as your break draws to a close. That excitement can fool you into thinking that it'll be easy to slip back into life as if nothing's changed.

What you'll find is that quite often, nothing *has* changed back home. What has changed is *you*. And as a result, even if the office, your colleagues and your friends seemed to have been almost frozen in time while you were away, the way you interact with them will have changed because you won't be quite the same. Just accept that this is normal, and give it some time. The same pull that makes the rat race so hard to exit will pull you back in soon enough.

Prepare to be Disengaged

While it's usually quite exciting to get together with friends and family when you return, don't be surprised if it's not quite the same for work. It can be very challenging to get back into gear when you first return. Depending on how you spent your time away, your job may seem unimportant, unstimulating, overstimulating or just plain *hard*. Don't worry—that's normal too, and it'll pass (or you'll find another job if it doesn't).

க

The best sabbaticals also make for the toughest reentries. A great escape can make for moments so close to perfection that it raises the bar to unattainable heights for your "normal" life.

If you have a tough time hitting your stride, then congratulations—it means you've had a taste of what a life lived deliberately can really be. And while the contrast can be rough, you can take solace in one fact:

You can always do it again.

Epilogue: *Paraguay*, South America

Certainly, travel is more than the seeing of sights; it is a change that goes on, deep and permanent, in the ideas of living.

-Miriam Beard

A S I WRITE THIS, I'm swinging in a hammock in central South America. It's Sunday, and we're taking some time off from the volunteer work we're doing at a refuge for homeless children. The coconut trees are waving in the breeze, and I can hear the strains of Latin music in the distance. It's so close to a perfect moment as to be stereotypical.

We're a long way from the Mayan temples of Guatemala, and the experiences that shaped the path to where we are now. As I reflect on trips of the past, and anticipate those of the future, I realize this sabbatical has been particularly rewarding—it's our first with children. The experience has been a tremendous one for our five year old daughter. I can hardly wait to take her on our next trip—an African odyssey when she turns ten. Shortly after our return home, we'll start the early planning stages—small, automatic bank withdrawals that will pay for the trip by the time it arrives five years from now.

As with all trips away, the clock is picking up speed now that we've settled into our life here. The days are ticking by and I know that soon it will be time to head home.

In this near-perfect moment, it's easy to remember why we worked so hard to get away. I know, though, that when we return, life will change, and it will be easy to forget these moments. It'll be easy to let *can't* and *shouldn't* back into our vocabulary. To find leaving far too hard, and staying far too easy.

It's hard for all of us to get away. After so many years and so many breaks, it's still challenging for us—I expect it will be for you, too. Don't give up. Your perfect moment is waiting for you. Imagine it, and hold tight to that vision.

Believe in yourself. The only thing that can stand in your way is you.

-Dan Clements
Paraguay, South America
2007

Recommended Reading

The 4-Hour Workweek: Escape 9-5, Live Anywhere, and Join the New Rich, Timothy Ferriss, Crown Publishers, 2007.

Six Months Off: How to plan, negotiate and take the break you need without burning bridges or going broke, Hope Dlugozima, James Scott, David Sharp, Henry Holt and Company, Inc., 1996.

In Praise of Slow: How a Worldwide Movement is Challenging the Cult of Speed, Carl Honoré, Vintage Canada, 2004.

Time off From Work: Using Sabbaticals to Enhance Your Life While Keeping Your Career on Track, Lisa Angowski Rogak, John Wiley & Sons, Inc., 1994.

Vagabonding: An Uncommon Guide to the Art of Long-Term World Travel, Rolph Potts, Villard, 2003.

Affluenza: The All-Consuming Epidemic, Second Edition, John DeGraaf, David Wann, Thomas H. Naylor, Berrett Koehler Publishers, 2005.
Rich Dad, Poor Dad, Robert Kiyosaki,

The E-Myth Revisited: Why Most Small Businesses Don't Work and What to Do About It, Michael E. Gerber, HarperCollins, 1995.

ENDNOTES

[1] *Affluenza: The All-Consuming Epidemic, Second Edition*, John DeGraaf, David Wann, Thomas H. Naylor, Berrett Koehler Publishers, 2005.

[2] Pamela Paul, "Time Out - more employees jump at chance to take a sabbatical", *American Demographics*, June 1, 2002. FindArticles.com. 02 Jan. 2007. http://www.findarticles.com/p/articles/mi_m4021/is_2002_June_1/ai_88679073

[3] 2007 survey of 1,281 UK workers commissioned by Norwich Union. http://www.aviva.com/index.asp?PageID=55&Year=2007&NewsID=3370

[4] The Hudson time off survey is based on a national poll of 2,082 U.S. workers conducted March 30 – April 2, 2007 and was compiled by Rasmussen Reports, LLC, an independent research firm. http://www.hudson-index.com/node.asp?SID=8085

[5] *The 4-Hour Workweek: Escape 9-5, Live Anywhere, and Join the New Rich*, Timothy Ferriss, Crown Publishers, 2007.

[6] *The Inner Game of Tennis*, Gallwey, W. Timothy, Random House Publishing, 1974.

[7] Yahoo! Finance/Harris Interactive survey, January 2007 in "Making the Most of the Money You Have" by Laura Rowley, Posted on Friday, January 19, 2007. http://finance.yahoo.com/expert/article/moneyhappy/21840; ylt=Am6Q94evvG 2LAR6Ki5kcPkgEwNIF

[8] *To the Limits: Pushing Yourself to the Edge-in Adventure and in Business*, Jim Clash, (John Wiley & Sons, 2003).

[9] Richardson, A. (1967a). Mental practice: A review and discussion. Part I. *Research Quarterly, 38.*

[10] *The 4-Hour Workweek: Escape 9-5, Live Anywhere, and Join the New Rich*, Timothy Ferriss, Crown Publishers, 2007.

[11] Pamela Paul "Time Out - more employees jump at chance to take a sabbatical", *American Demographics*, June 1, 2002. FindArticles.com. 02 Jan. 2007. http://www.findarticles.com/p/articles/mi_m4021/is_2002_June_1/ai_88679073

[12] Marilyn Gardner, "Bosses See Benefit In Giving Sabbaticals To Workers", *Christian Science Monitor*, September 24, 2007.

[13] *The Earth is Flat: A Brief History of the Twenty-first Century*, Thomas J. Friedman, Picador, 2007.

[14] *Rich Dad's Cashflow Quadrant*, Robert Kiyosaki, Business Plus, 2000.

[15] *Six Months Off: How to plan, negotiate and take the break you need without burning bridges or going broke.* Hope Dlugozima, James Scott, David Sharp, Henry Holt and Company, Inc., 1996.

[16] *The Two-Income Trap: Why Middle-Class Mothers and Fathers are Going Broke*, Elizabeth Warren, Amelia Warren Tyagi, Basic Books, 2003.

[17] *In Praise of Slow: How a Worldwide Movement is Challenging the Cult of Speed*, Carl Honoré, Vintage Canada, 2004.

ABOUT THE AUTHORS

DAN CLEMENTS writes and speaks on health, business, and work-life balance. To learn more about his books, visit www.danclements.com.

TARA GIGNAC, ND is a speaker and Naturopathic Doctor in private practice in Collingwood, Ontario, Canada. For more information on Tara's books and practice, visit www.taragignac.com.

Together, they've taken numerous sabbaticals around the world, including Mexico, Central America, South America, South East Asia, Australia, New Zealand and more. And they've done it all while juggling mortgages, kids, jobs and businesses.

Their next escape will be to Africa.

Share Your Escape Stories!

You can contact Dan and Tara, get escape advice, and share your sabbatical stories and book feedback at the *Escape 101* website:
www.escape-101.com

CPSIA information can be obtained
at www.ICGtesting.com
Printed in the USA
LVHW051051030622
720439LV00003B/372